SWEET & LOVELY

A satirical look at life and love...Volume 1

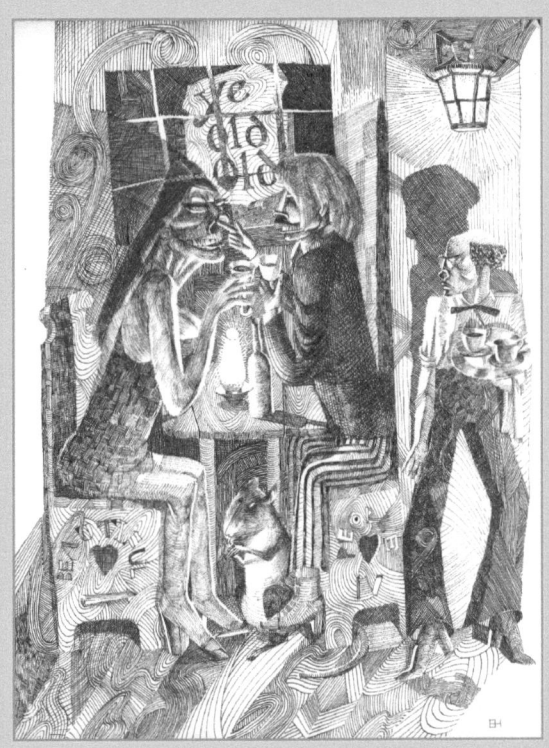

Edward Henrion

Ed Henrion's Razor Line Cuts to the Core of our Common Depravity

essay by Ed McCormack

If most artists are said to have a muse, it might be assumed that the satirical draftsman Ed Henrion has an imp that hops out of an ink bottle like Ko-Ko the Clown in those vintage black and white animated cartoons of the 1920s. In captivity for over half a century, that demonic imp has finally emerged with a vengeance in the present volume, at the persistent urging –– one might even call it nudging –– of Henrion's wife, the well-known fiber artist Marilyn Henrion.

While Ed masqueraded for many years as a mild-mannered high school art teacher at Erasmus High School in Brooklyn, the couple were steeped in the lively downtown art and literary scene of the '60s and '70s. They held regular salons in their Greenwich Village apartment where Allen Ginsberg, Philip Lamantia, Ray Bremser, and other Beat Generation luminaries read poetry, avant gardists such as Jackson Maclow performed, and their social set included visual artists such as Joseph Cornell, Tom Wesselman, and Claus Oldenburg, in whose happenings Marilyn performed.

But aside from contributing a few freelance editorial illustrations to small publications such as Human Events and Libertarian Review, Ed (apparently a retiring man long before he retired) wanted no part of the art business per se.

This despite having been a regular, along with de Kooning, Rothko, Motherwell, and other big guns of the New York School, at the legendary Artists Club on 8th Street in the 1950s, and having, for a time, painted large canvases in the manner of a latter-day Matisse (whom he has come to resemble, with his owlish specs and white beard, in recent years).

It would seem that the distance Ed Henrion has kept from the grubby, hustling aspects of the art scene has served his graphic vision well, giving him the freedom to skewer aspects of the cultural establishment that might be off-limits to a more professionally ambitious satirist. Not even that once vaunted arbiter of Hip, The Village Voice, was safe from his acid-etched pen-line, judging from one scathing drawing of a flamboyantly foppish critic / commentator in high-heeled pumps posturing at his typewriter, while multi-culti artsy-fartsy wannabes salivate at a window bearing the paper's familiar logo like Oliver Twist ogling the porridge. And doesn't that little cutie in the diaper, sucking on a pacifier and clutching a stuffed teddy bear in another drawing, bear a suspicious resemblance to Picasso?

Other personal acquaintances and / or cultural icons such as Allen Ginsberg or Jascha Heifetz may occasionally put in cameo appearances –– rarely in flattering roles. (Could that dandyish dude studying the funky folk singers in Washington Square as if they were bedbugs under a microscope be none other than the natty New Journalist Tom Wolfe?) But it's never necessary to recognize them in order to appreciate these drawings for their own wicked virtues. For, even when likenesses, or details suggest a particular time period, these pictures are never merely topically obvious in the manner of a political cartoon. Rather, they attack the larger, more timeless and universal themes of human nature in a more elusive, enigmatic way that puts Henrion on a par, for both his breadth of vision and his draftsmanly abilities, with better-known graphic satirists such as Gerald Scarfe and his draftsmanly abilities, Ralph Steadman and Tomi Ungerer. For surely Henrion's figurative distortions are as wildly inventive and over the top as those of the two British artists, Scarfe and Steadman (if more intricately filled with linear swirls and crosshatching in a style suggesting Edward Gorey on acid), and his delight in depicting kinky erotic fetishes equals that of the Frenchman Ungerer.

When Henrion ventures into color (mostly in what looks to be watercolor, gouache, colored pencil, or pastel, combined with that always incisive ink or graphite line), hints of the fine painter he once was are clearly evident. But as with George Grosz (the master to whom he, like all the other terrific draftsman mentioned in this appreciation, is most beholden), it is in a razor-sharp line, cutting to the core of our common depravity, that Ed Henrion finds his true métier.

*   *   *

Ed McCormack, one of the original contributing editors of Andy Warhol's Interview and a former feature writer and columnist for Rolling Stone, co-publishes the New York art journal Gallery & Studio with his wife, Jeannie McCormack. He is also author of an upcoming memoir, "Hoodlum Heart".

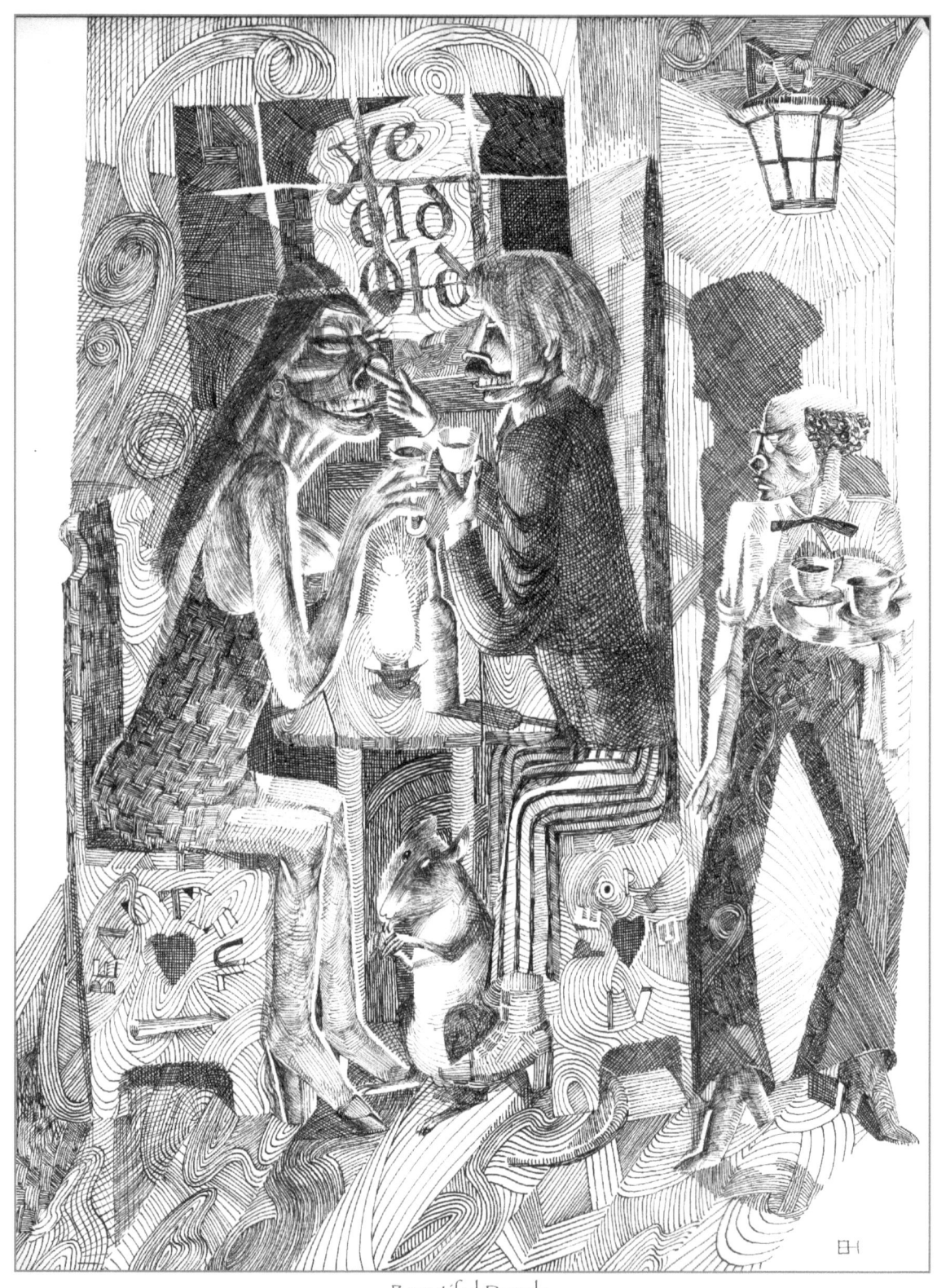

Beautiful People

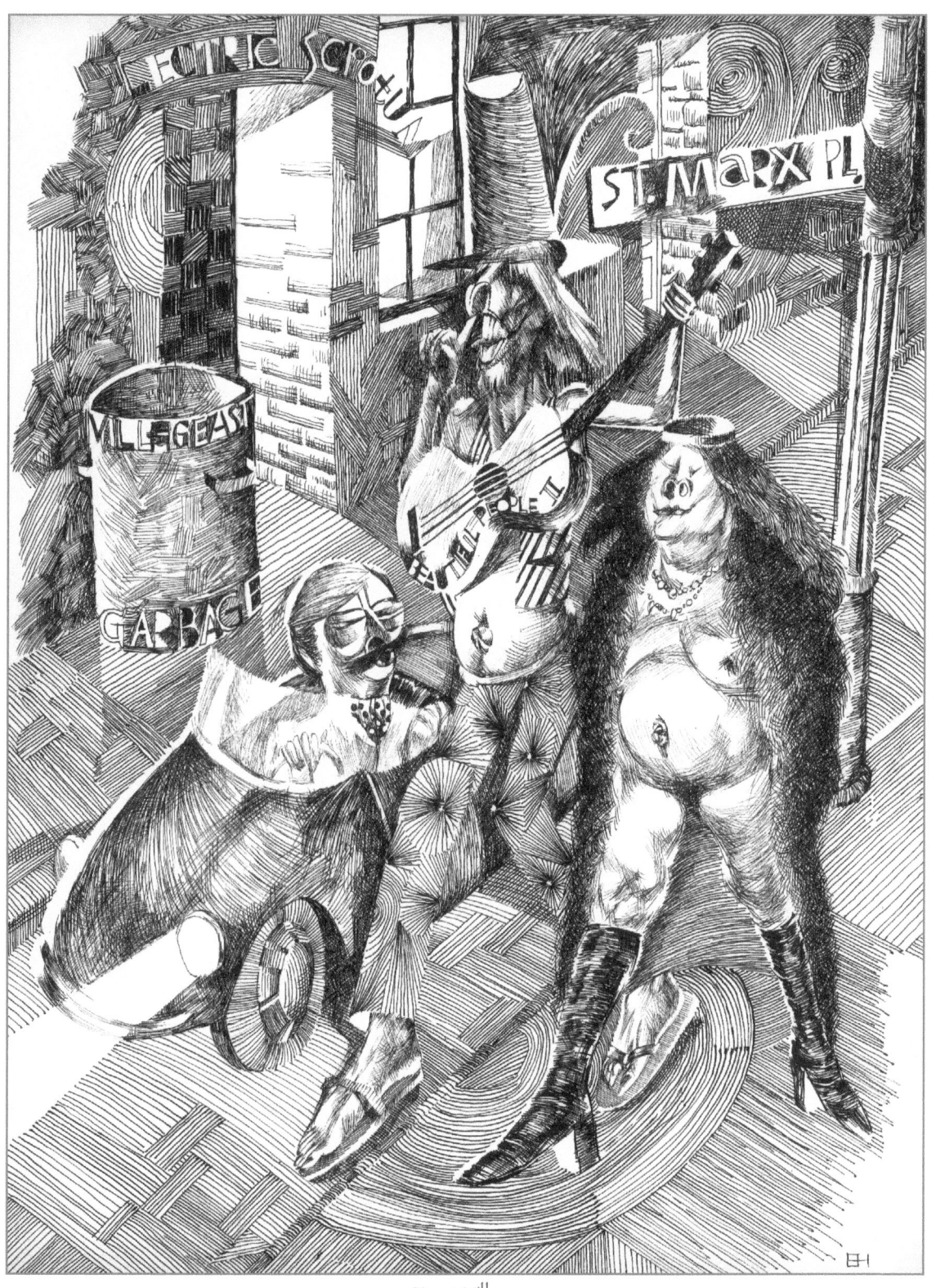

East Village

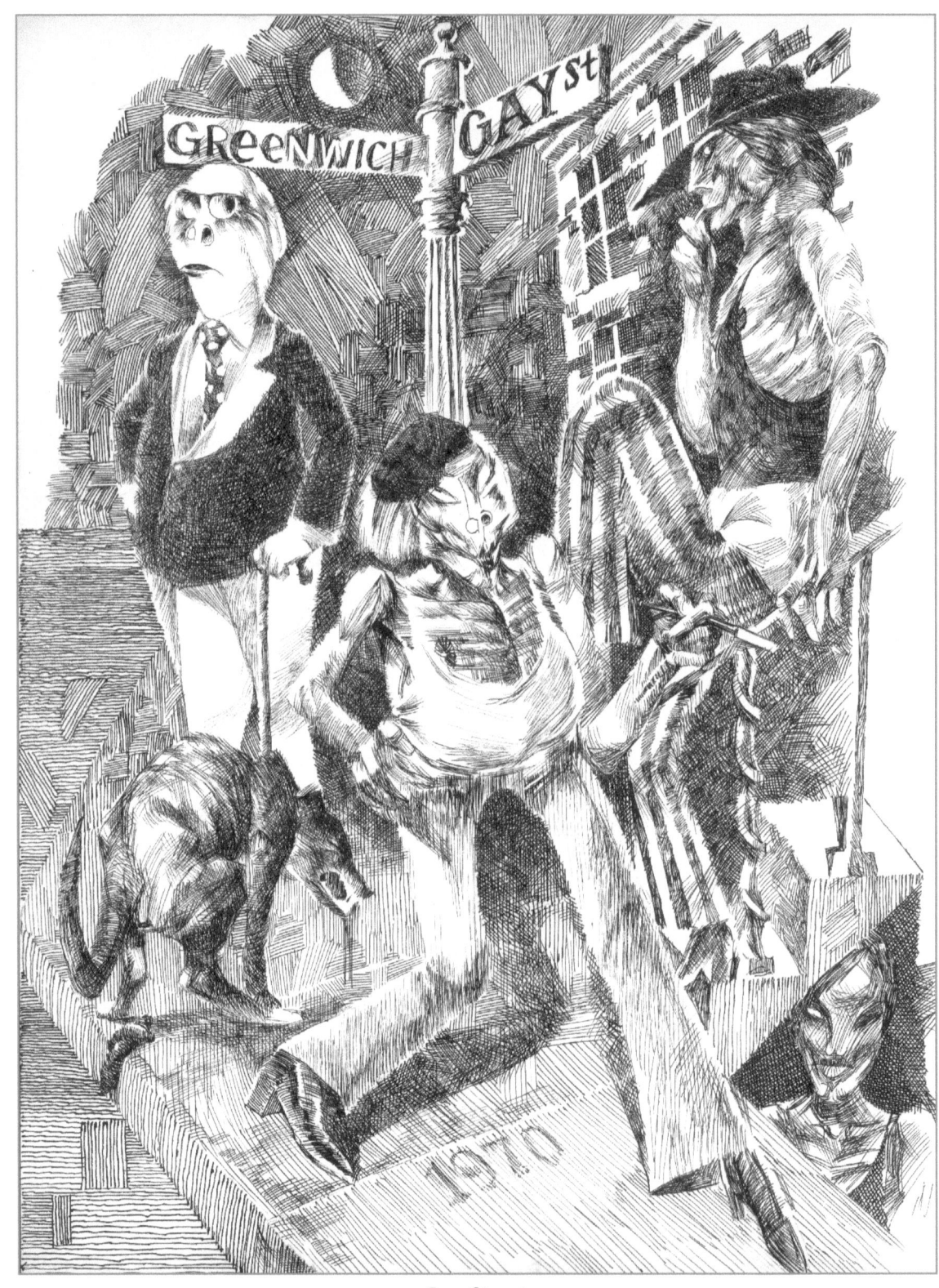

Gay Street

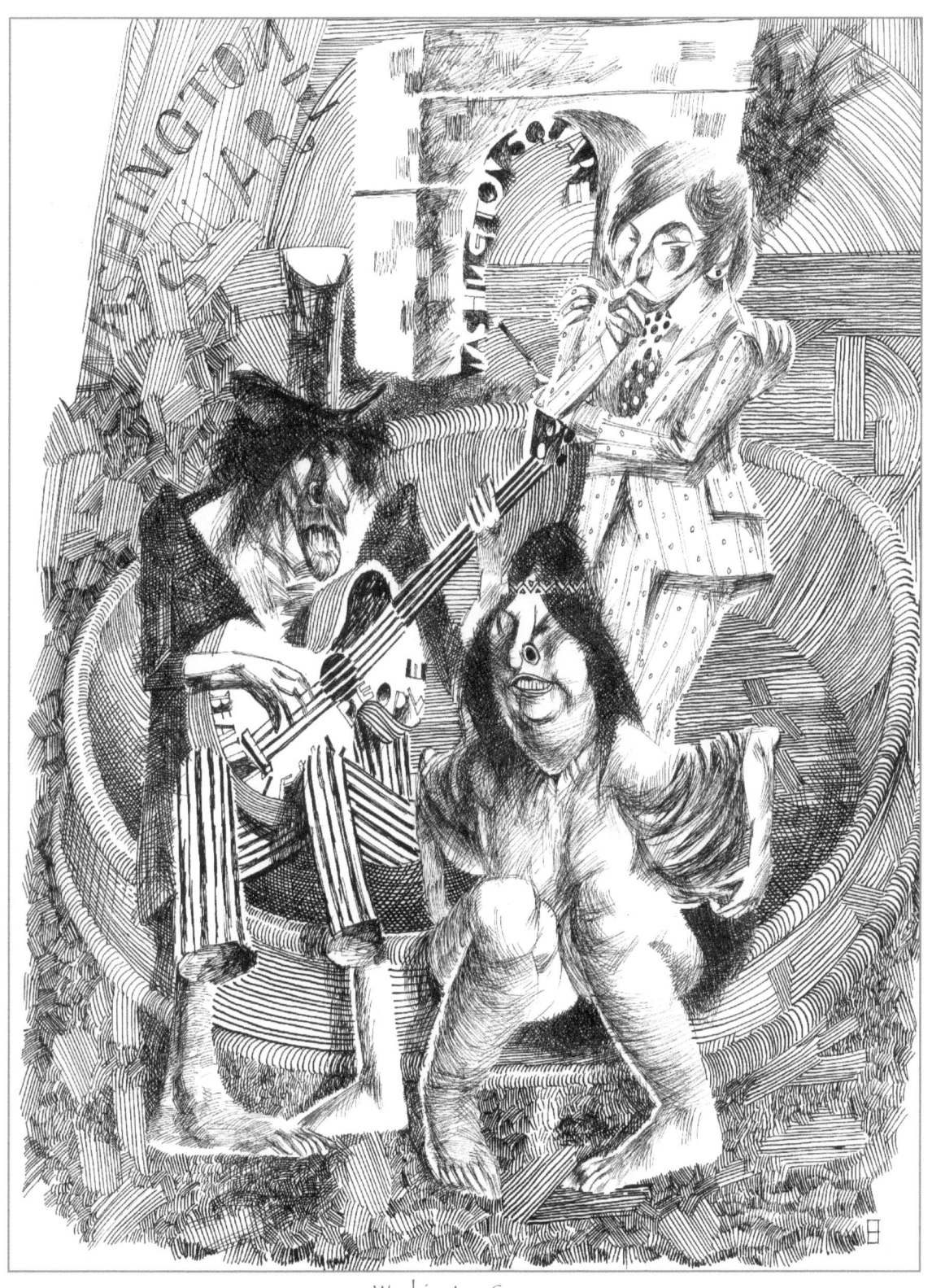

Washington Square

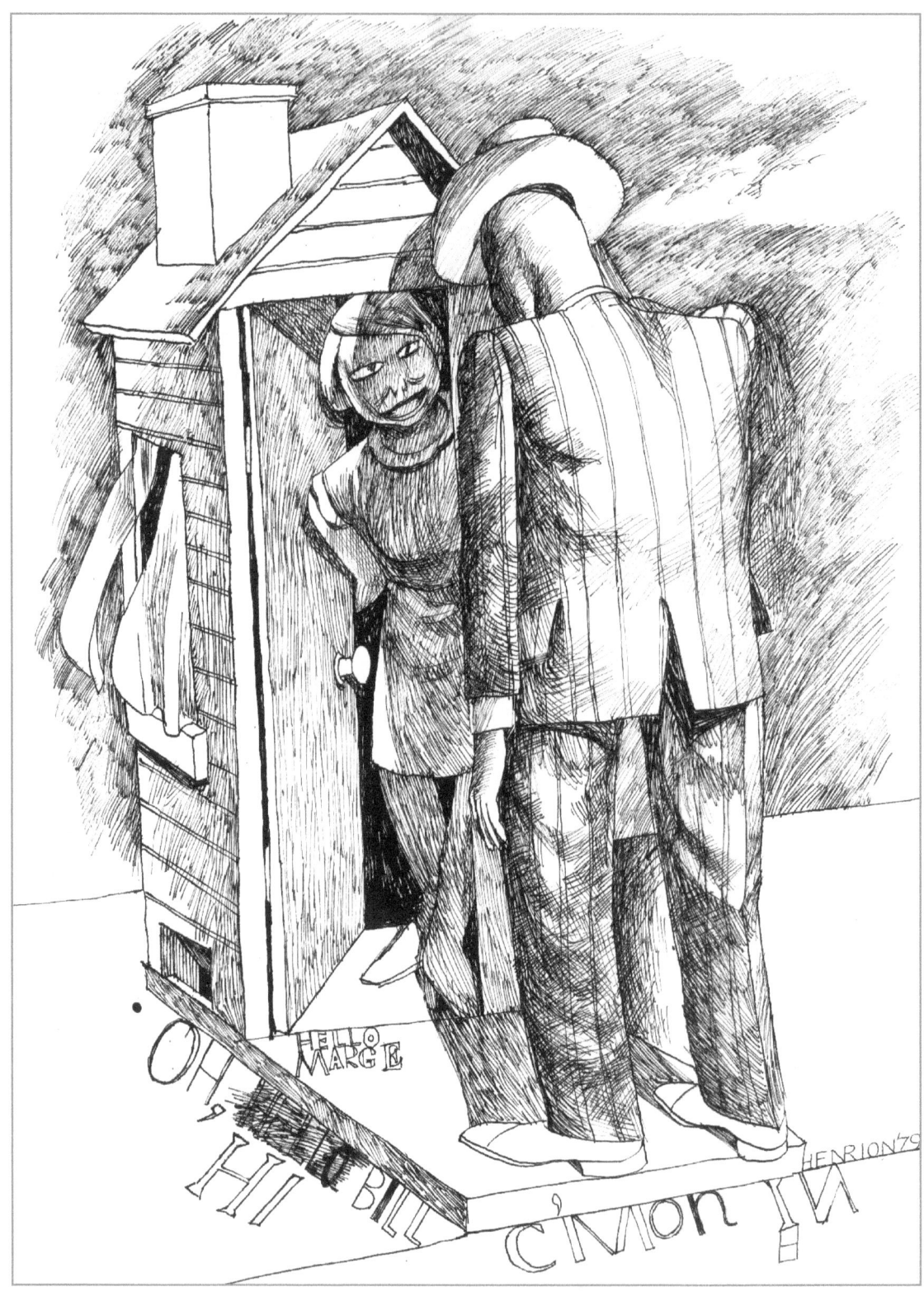

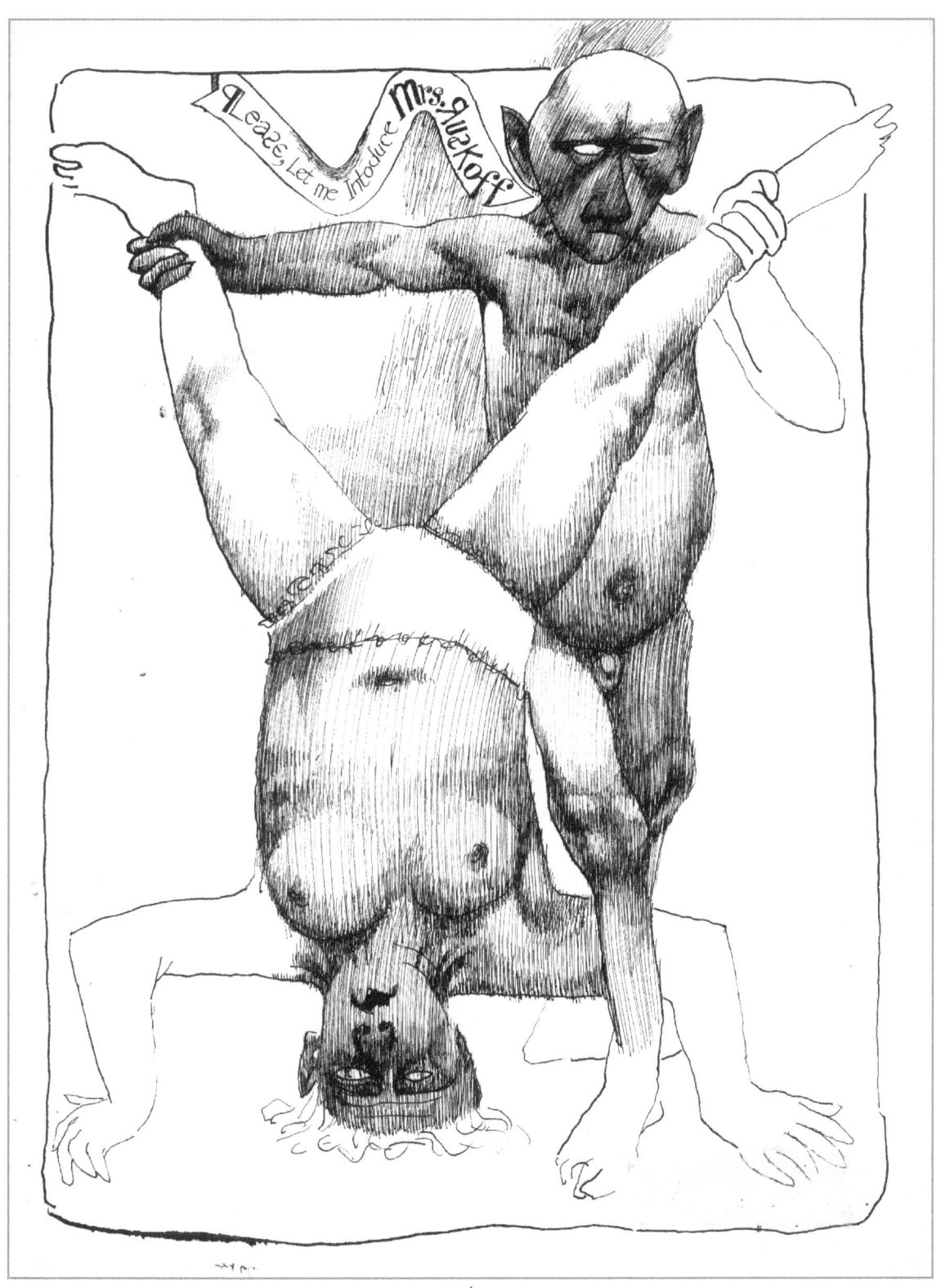

Introduction

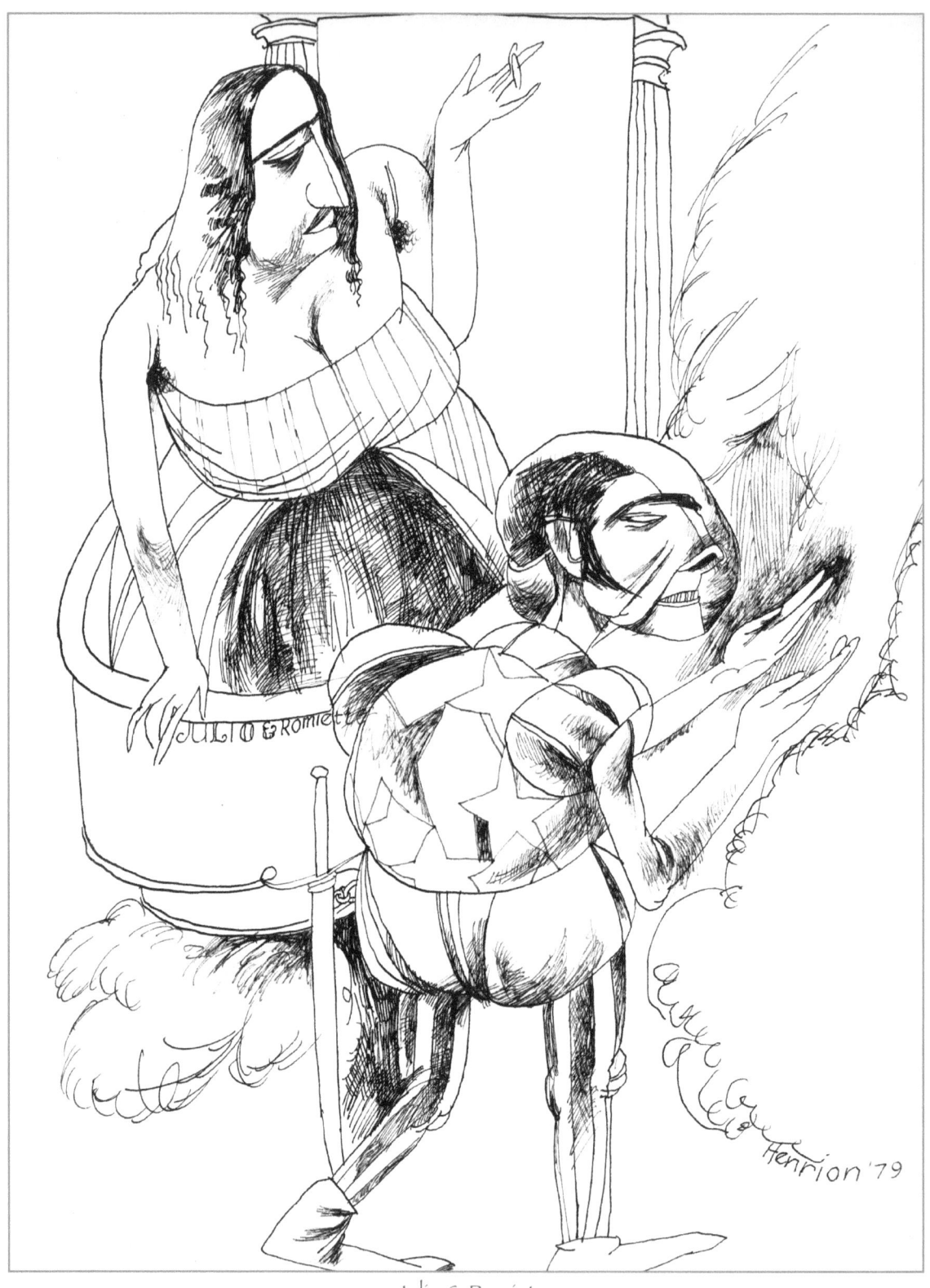

Julio & Romiet

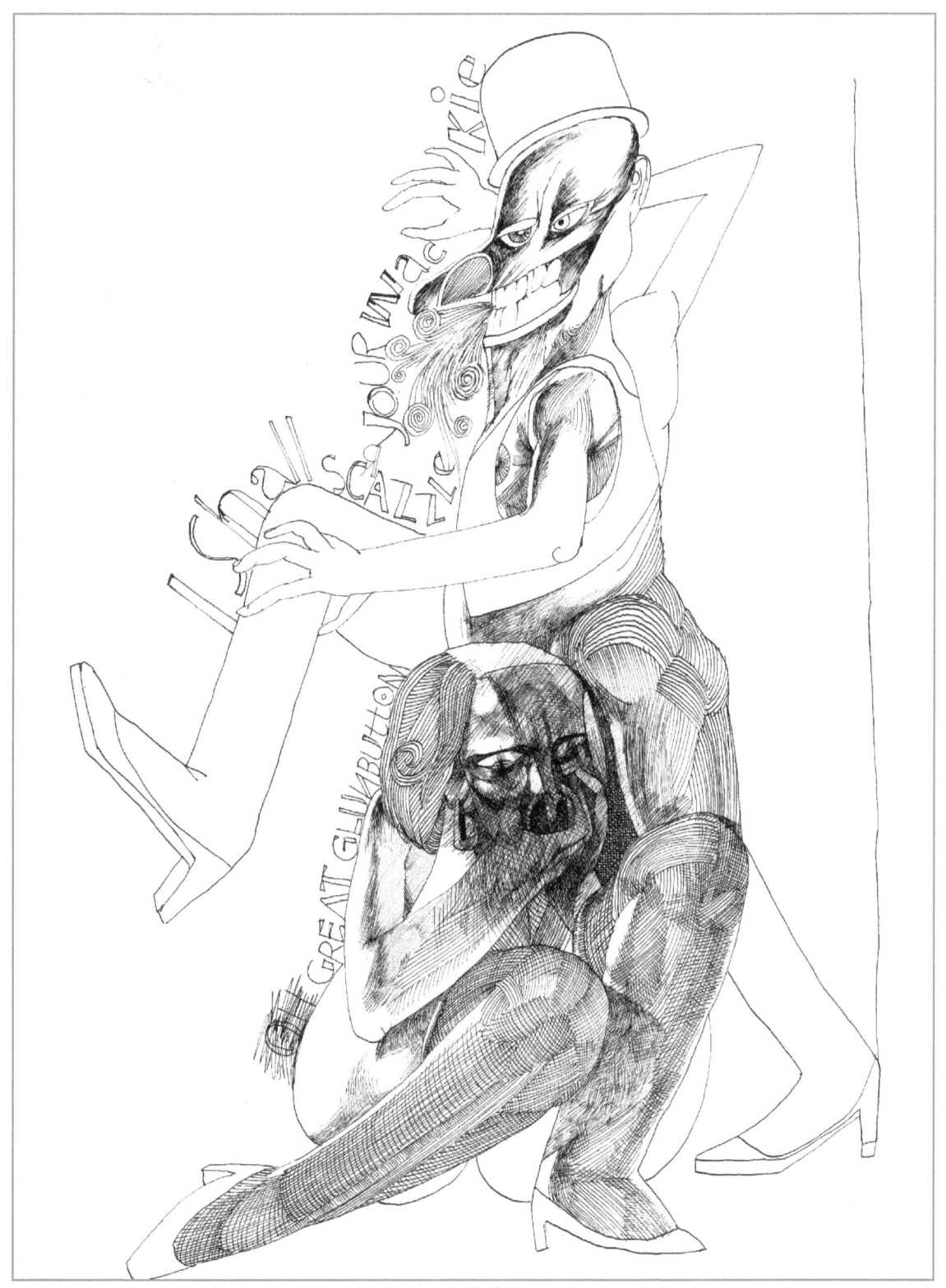

I Shall

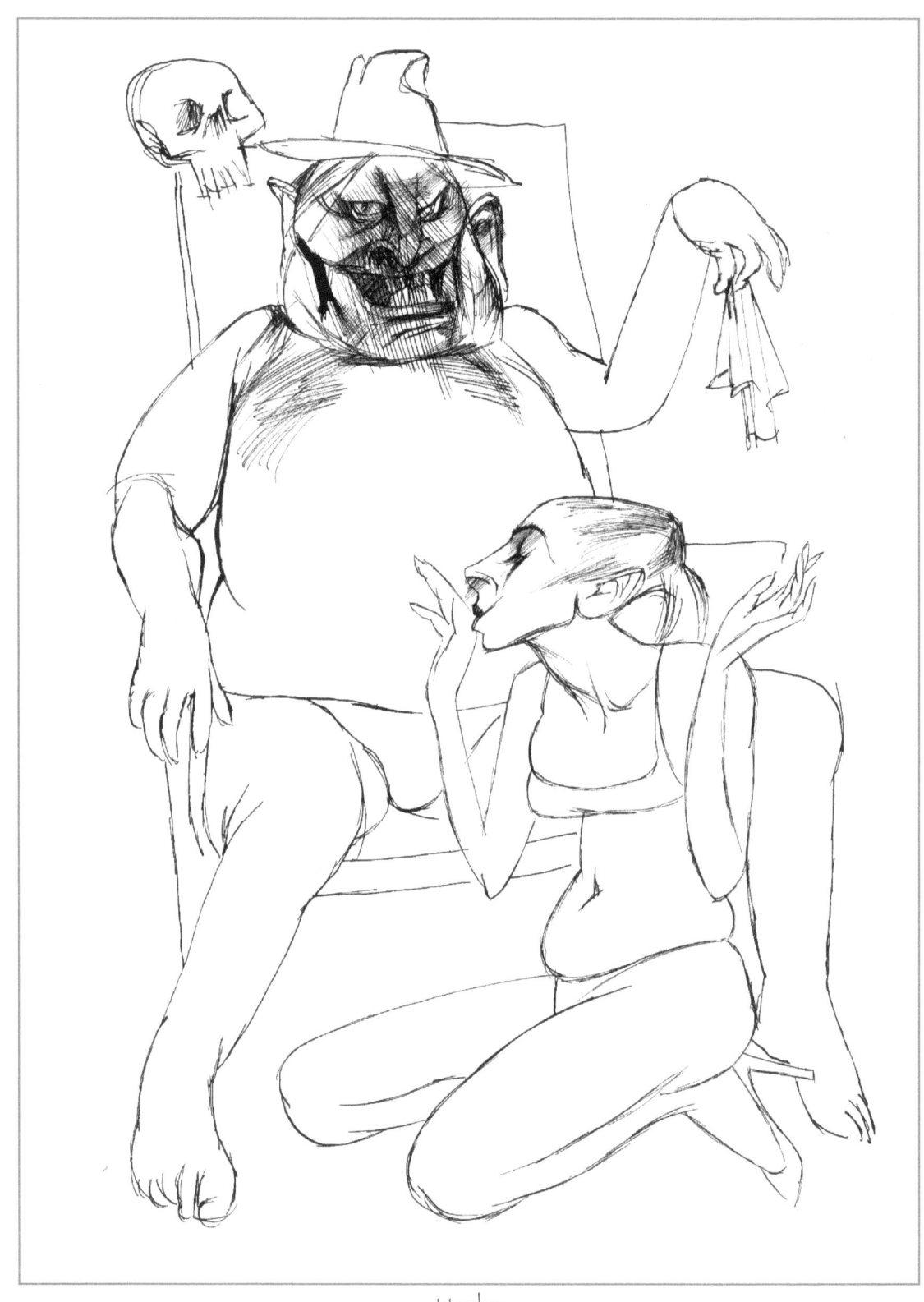

Hanky

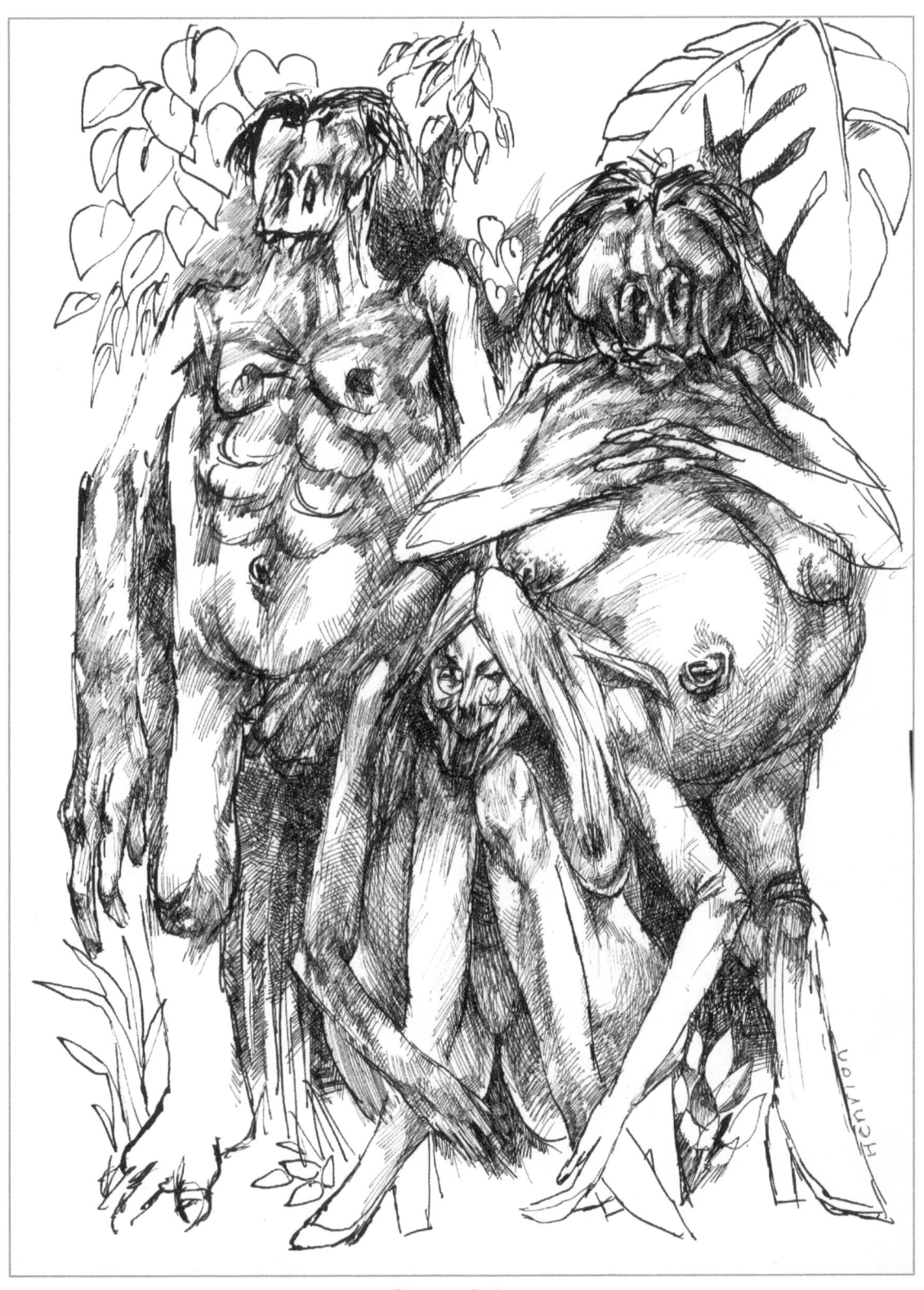

Tarzan & Jane

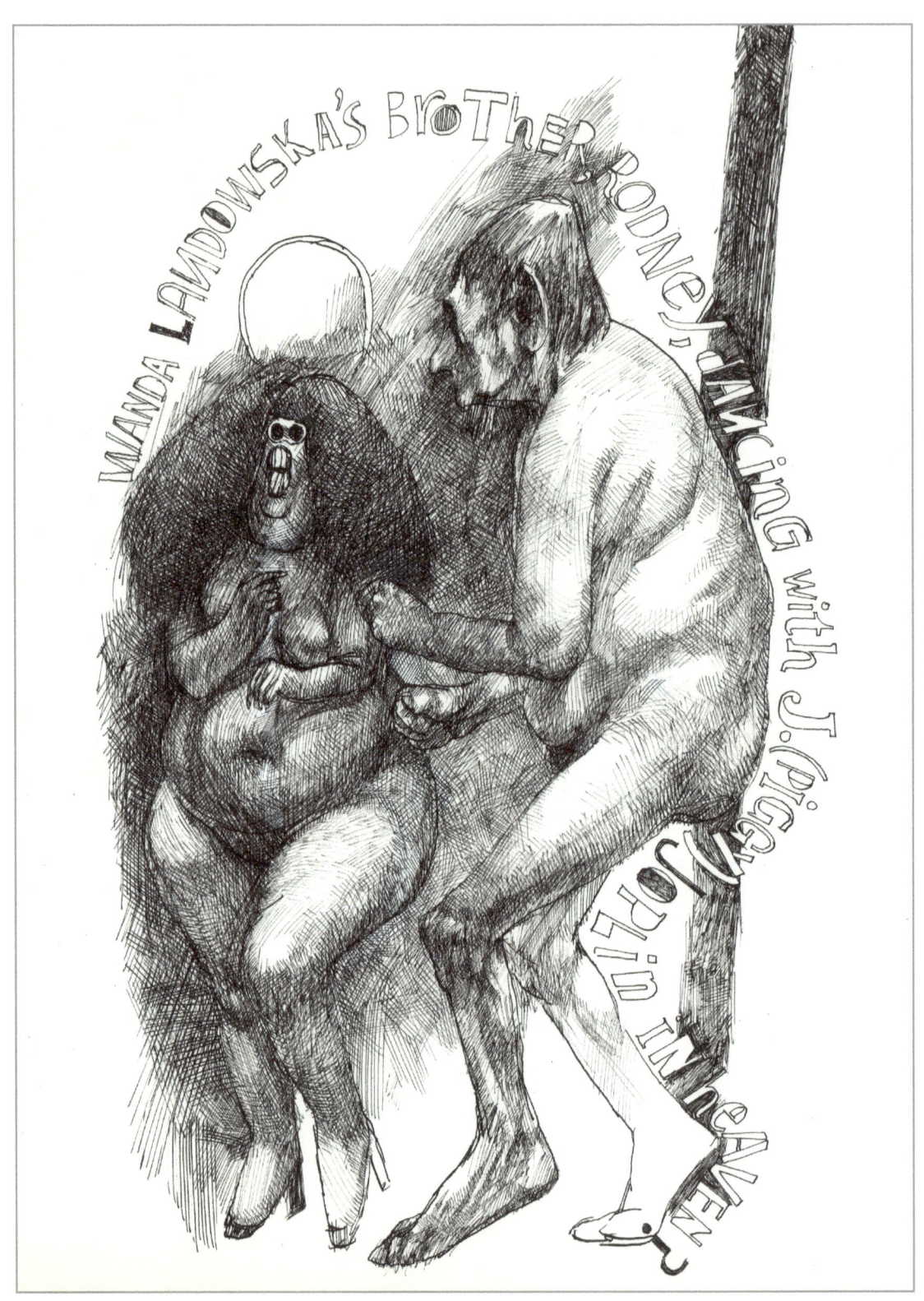

Dancing In Heaven

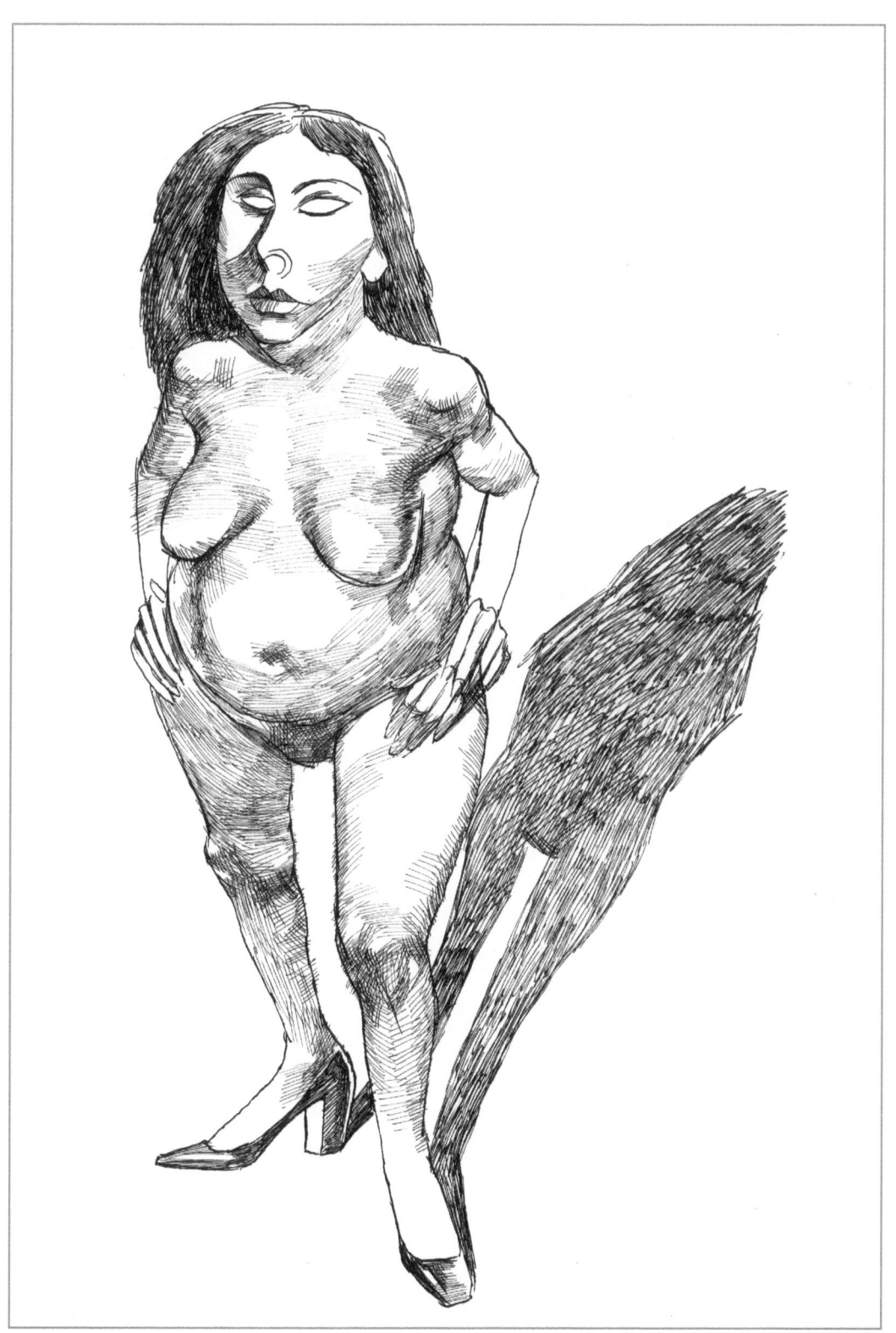

Woman With Shadow

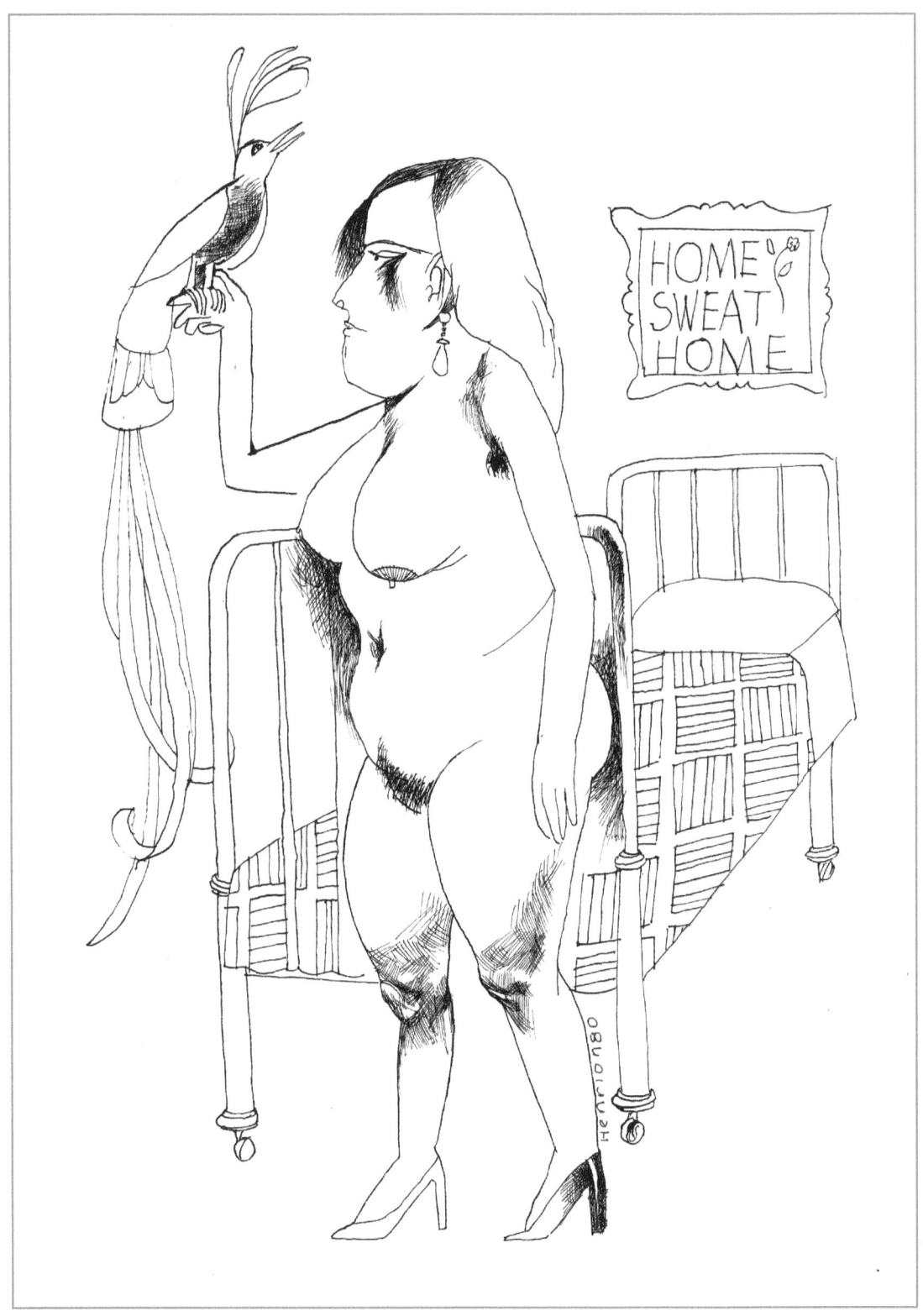

Home

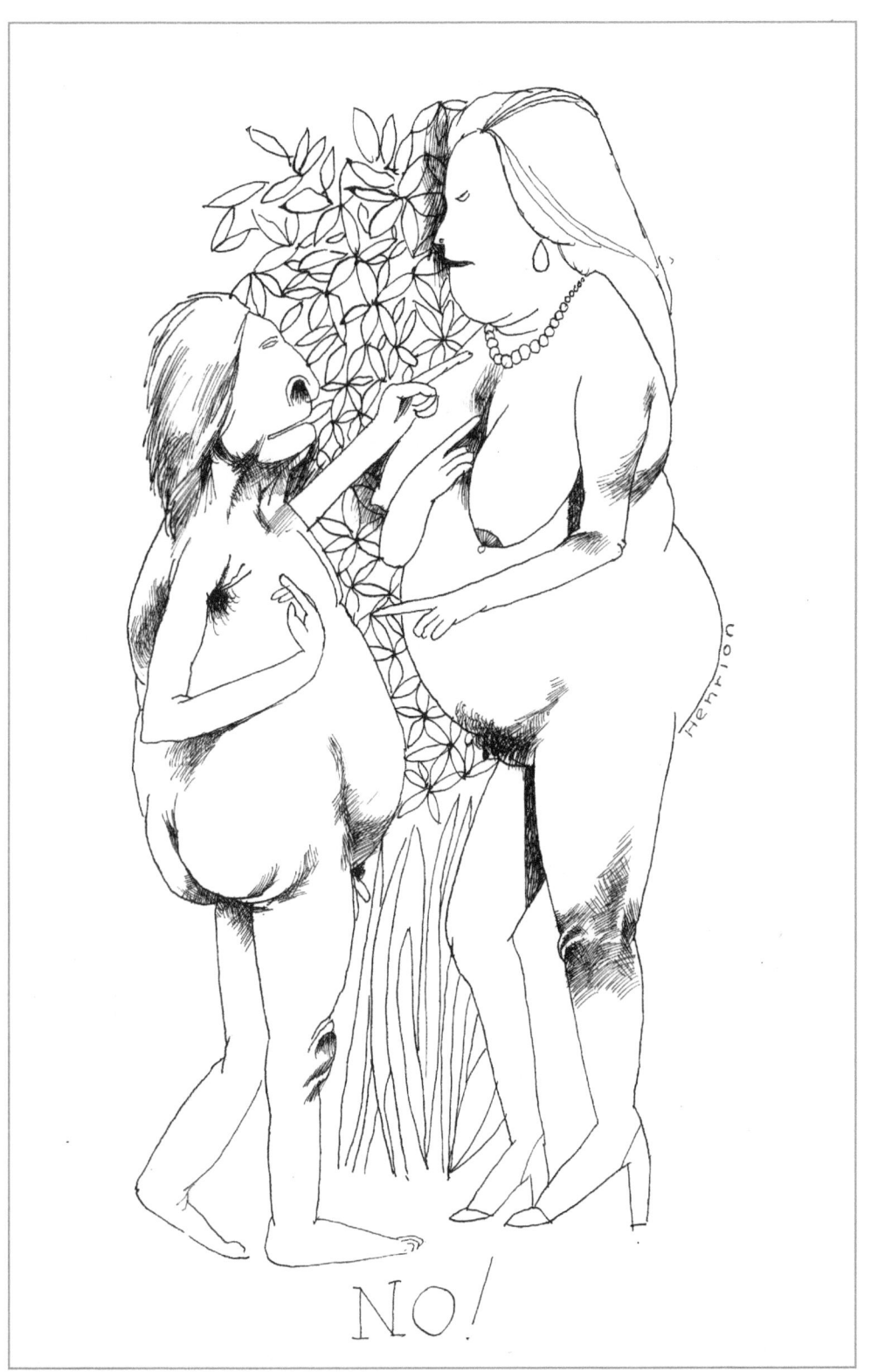

No

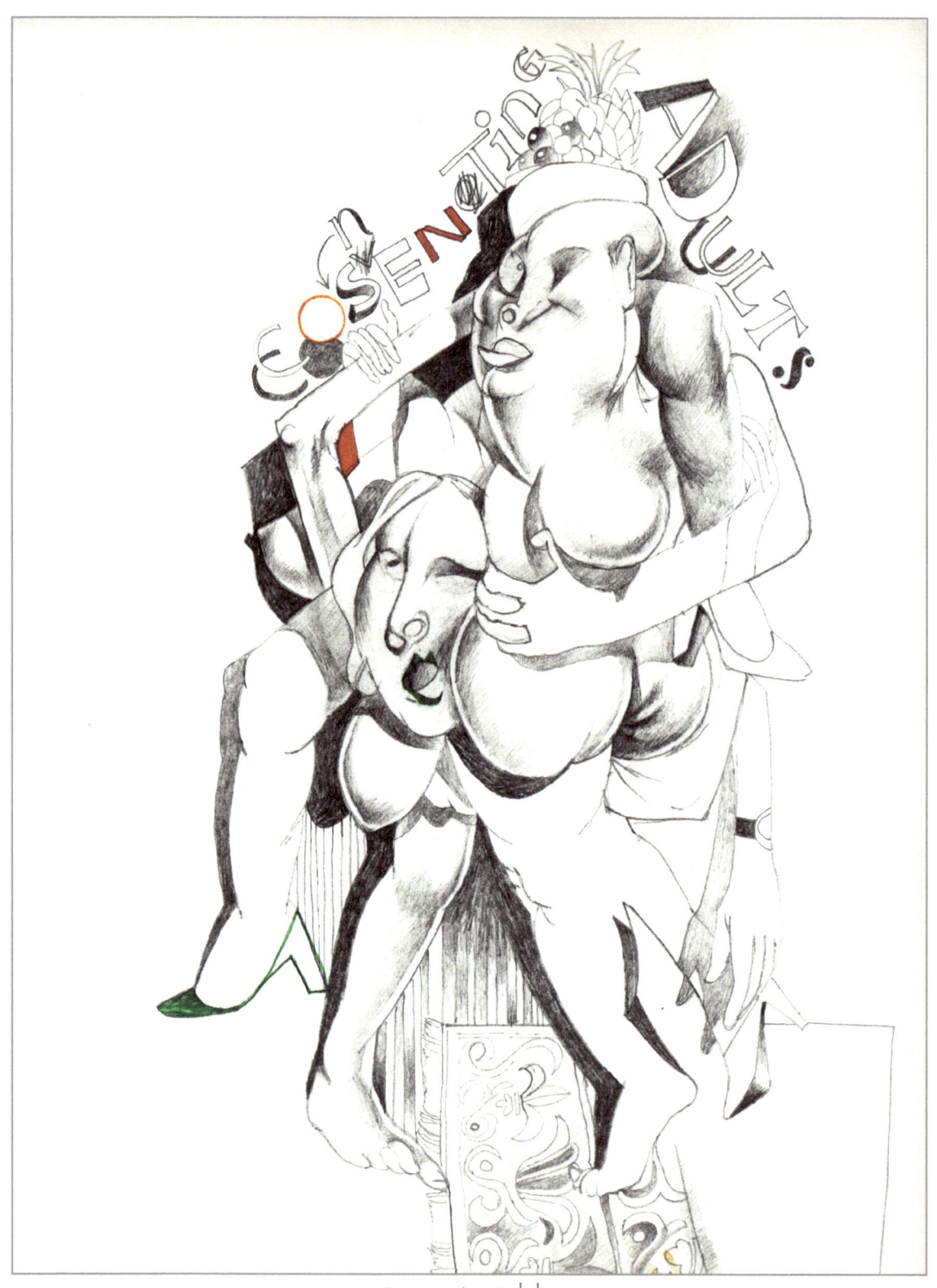

Consenting Adults

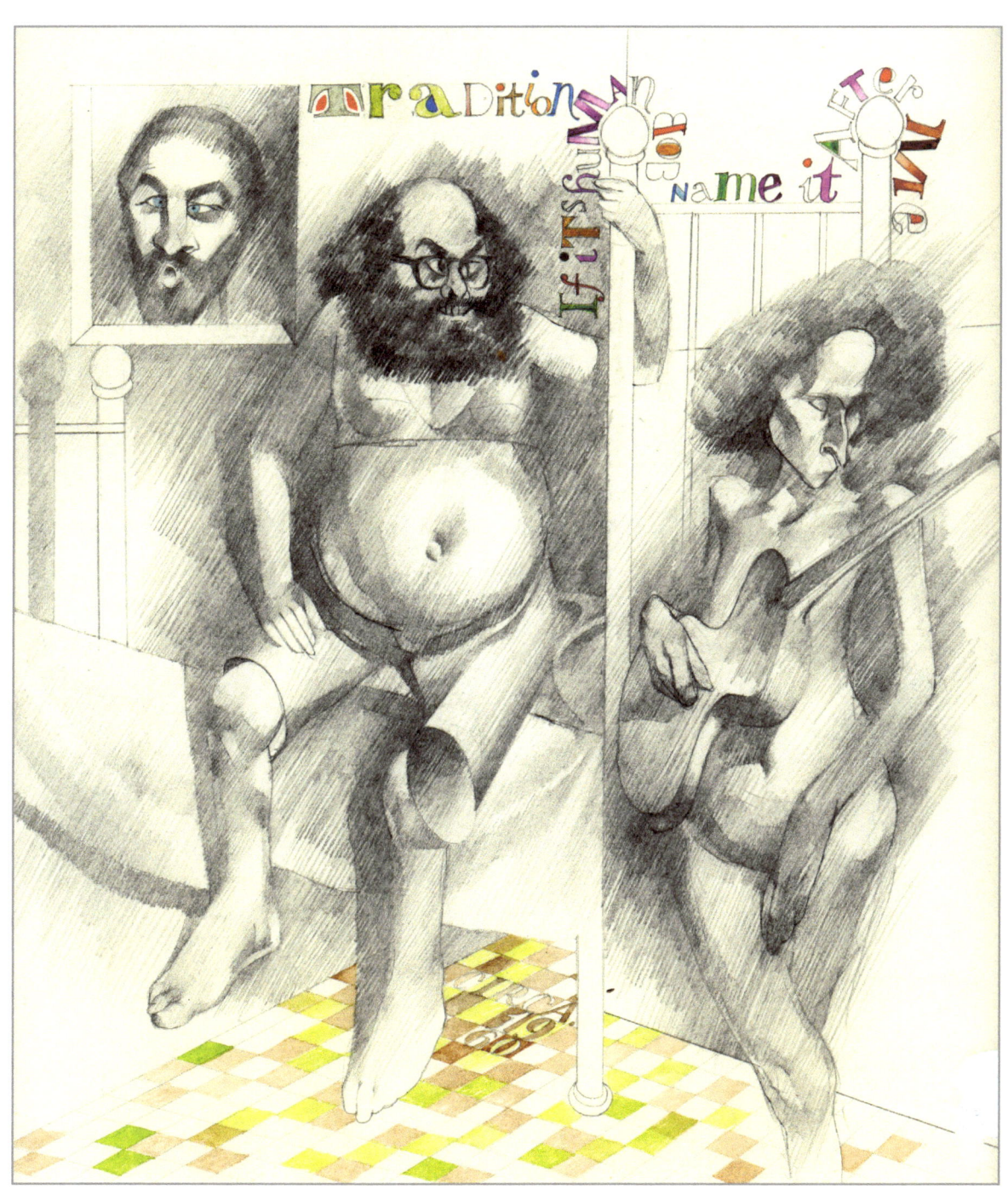

Ginsberg & Dylan

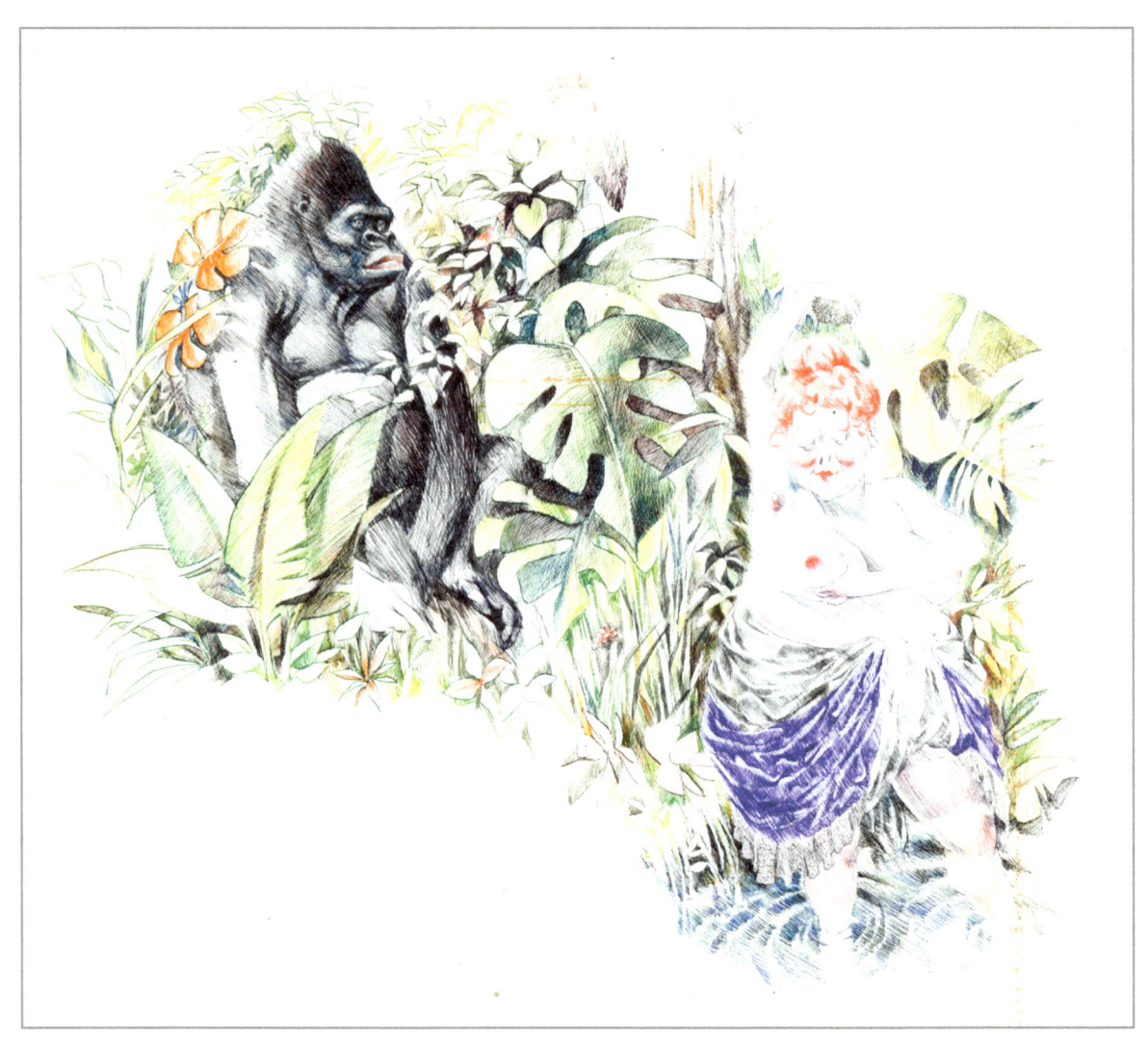

Adam & Eve

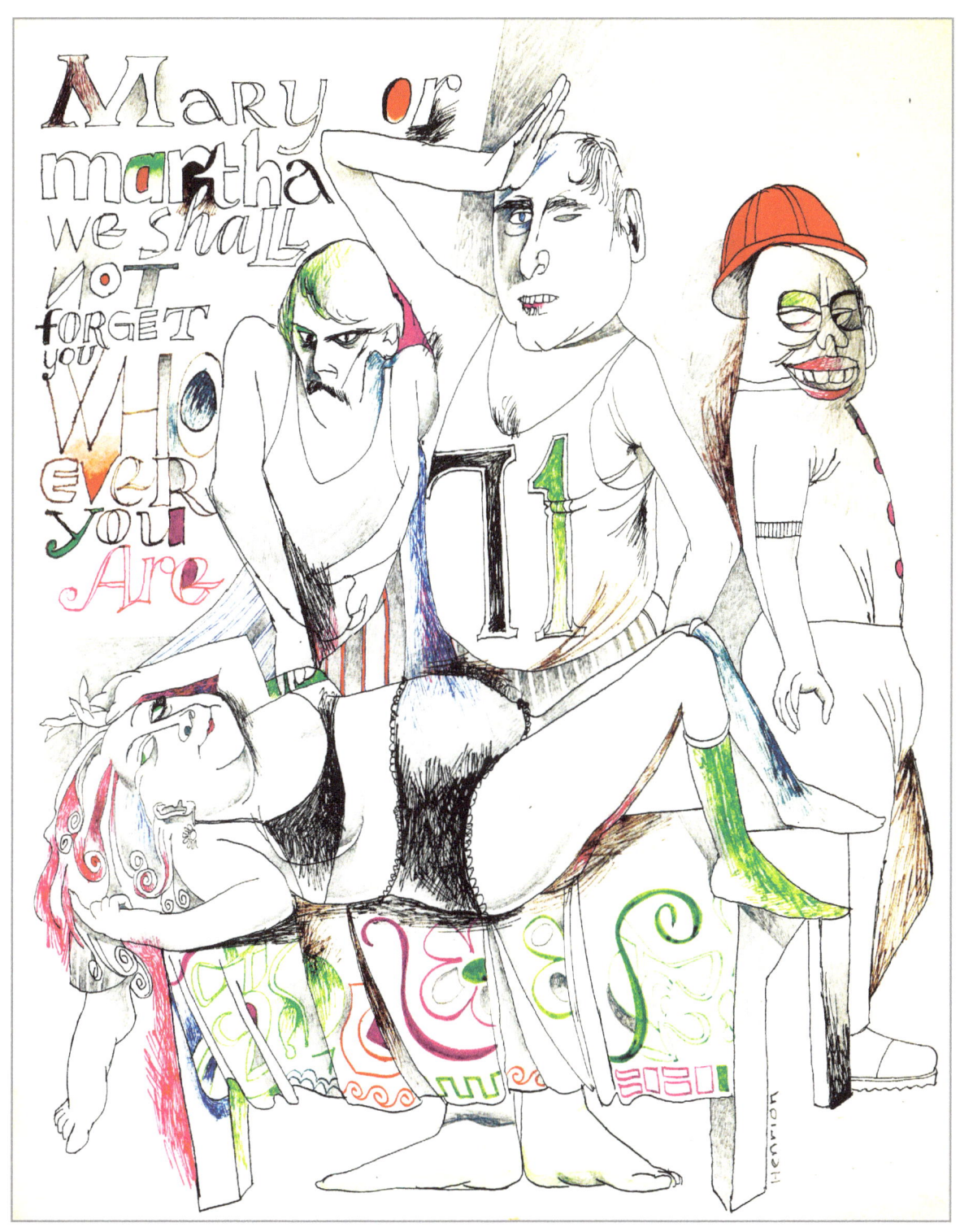

We Shall Not Forget

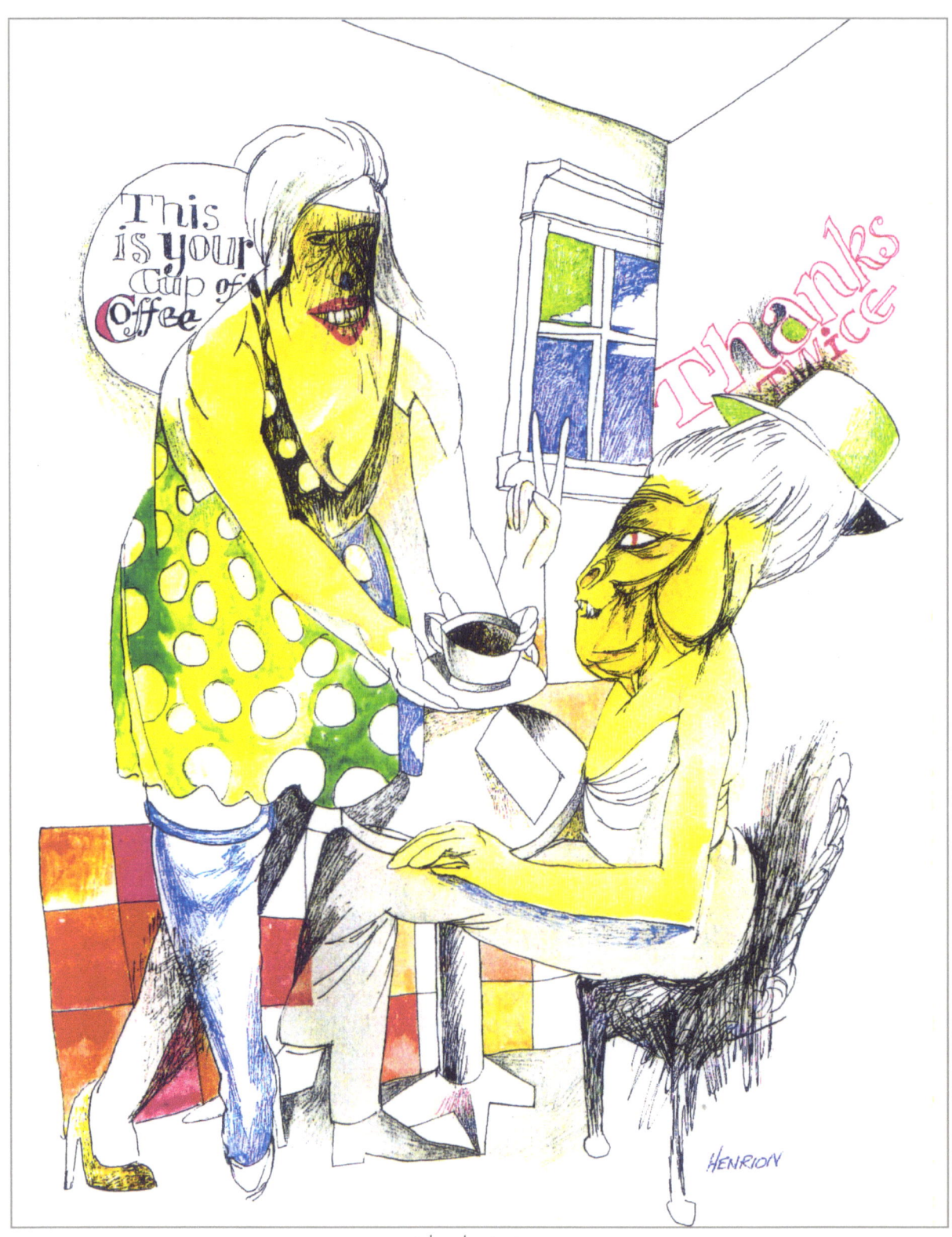

Thanks Twice

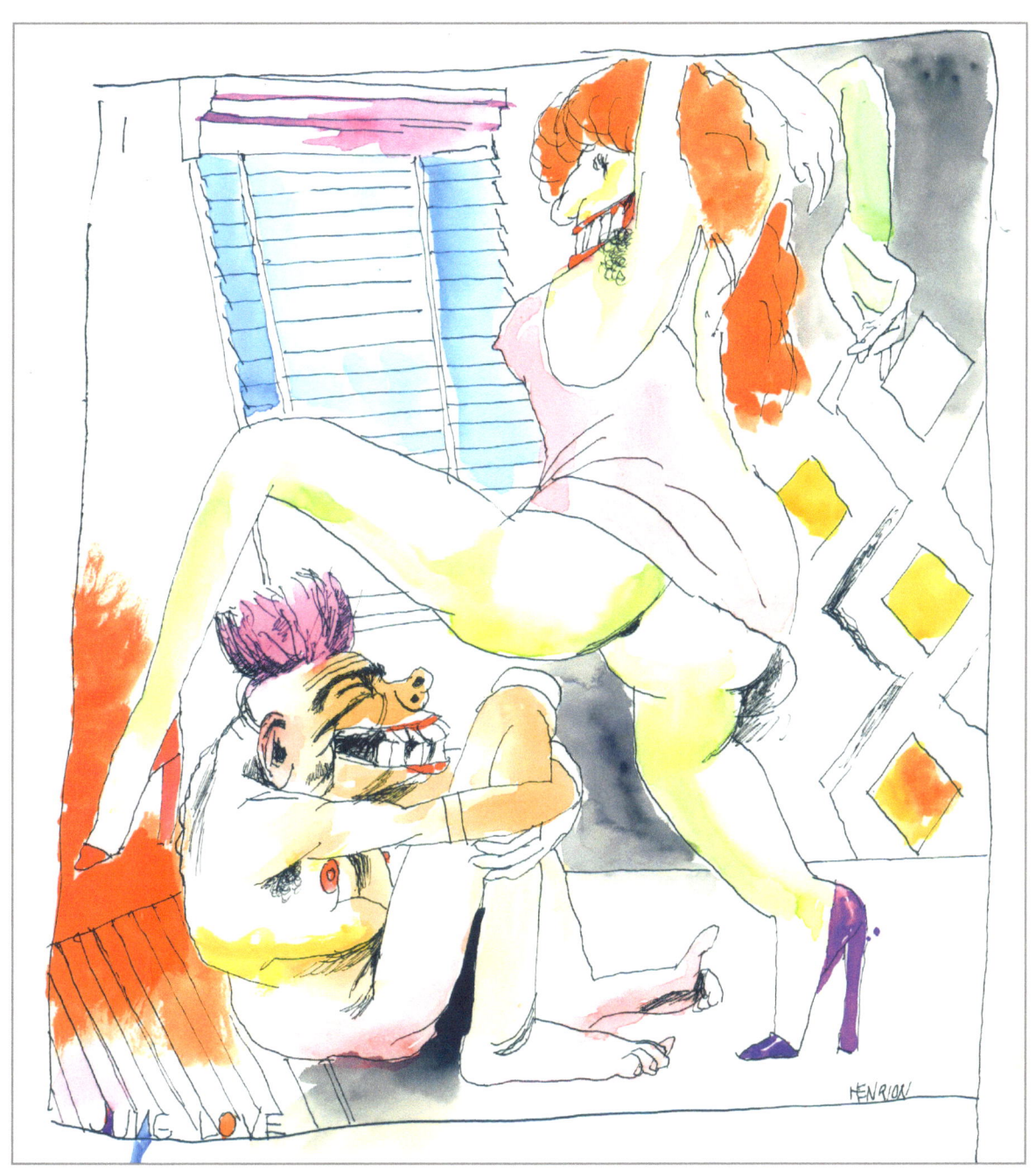

Jung Love

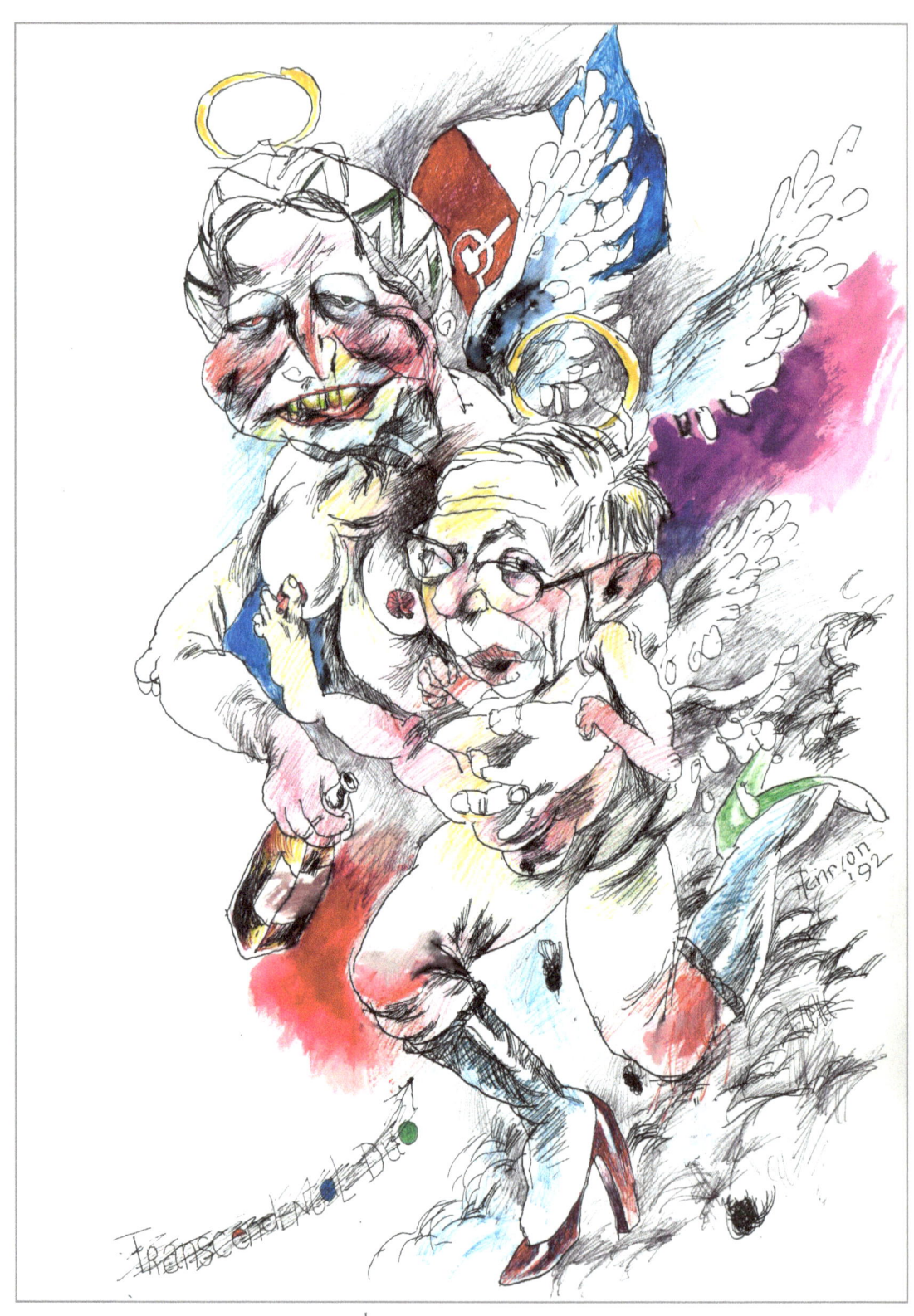

de Beauvoir & Sartre

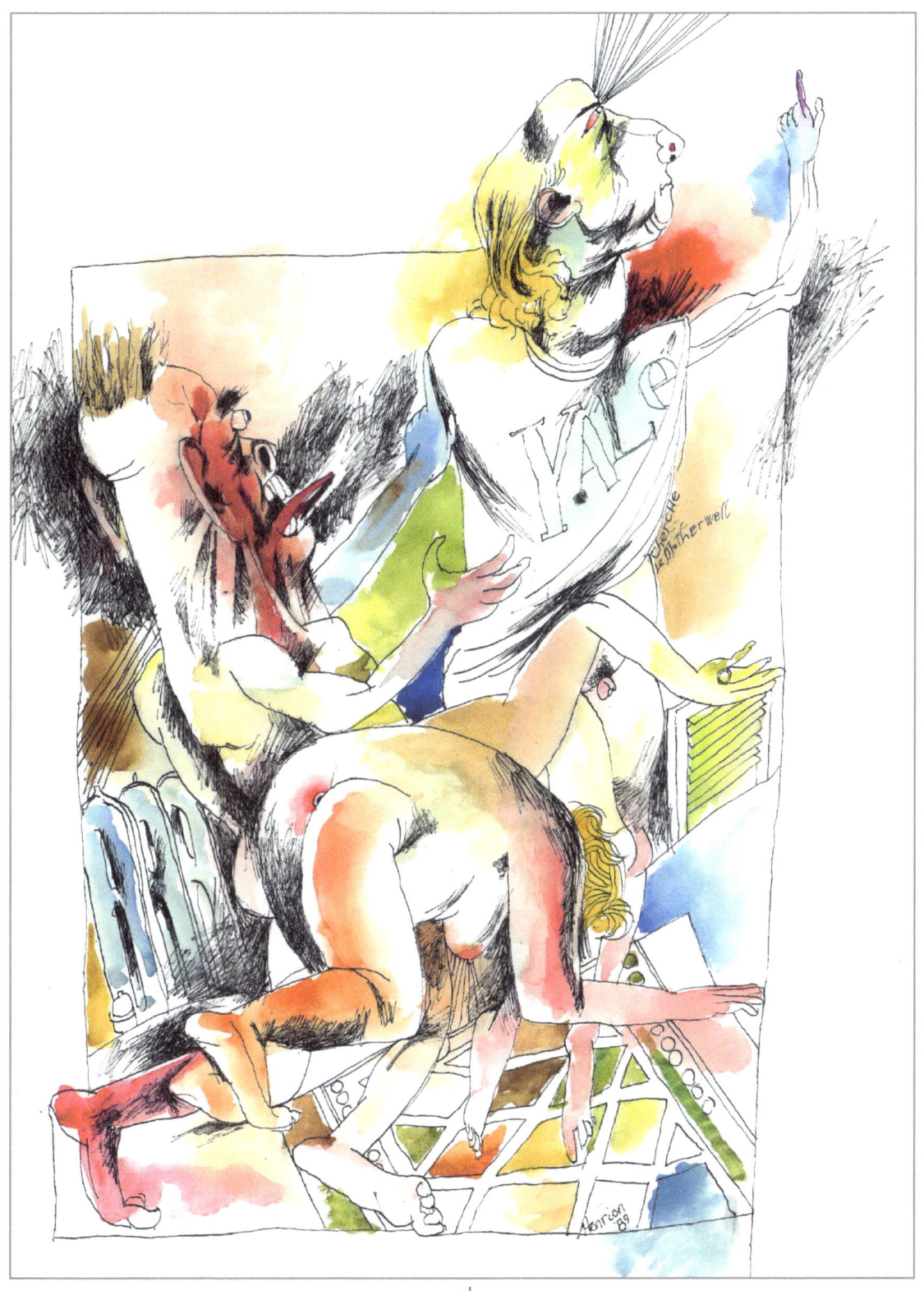

Yale

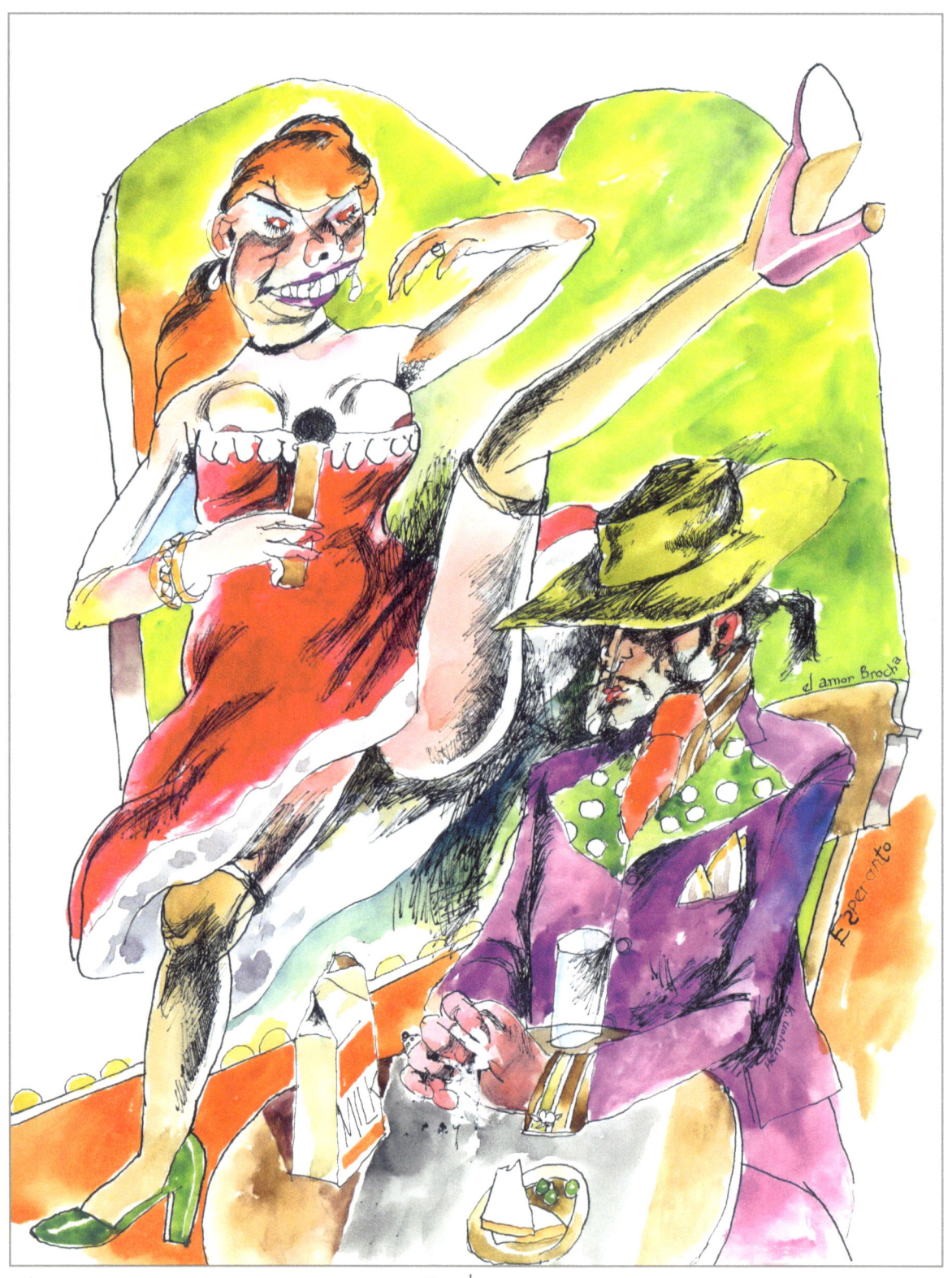

Fandango

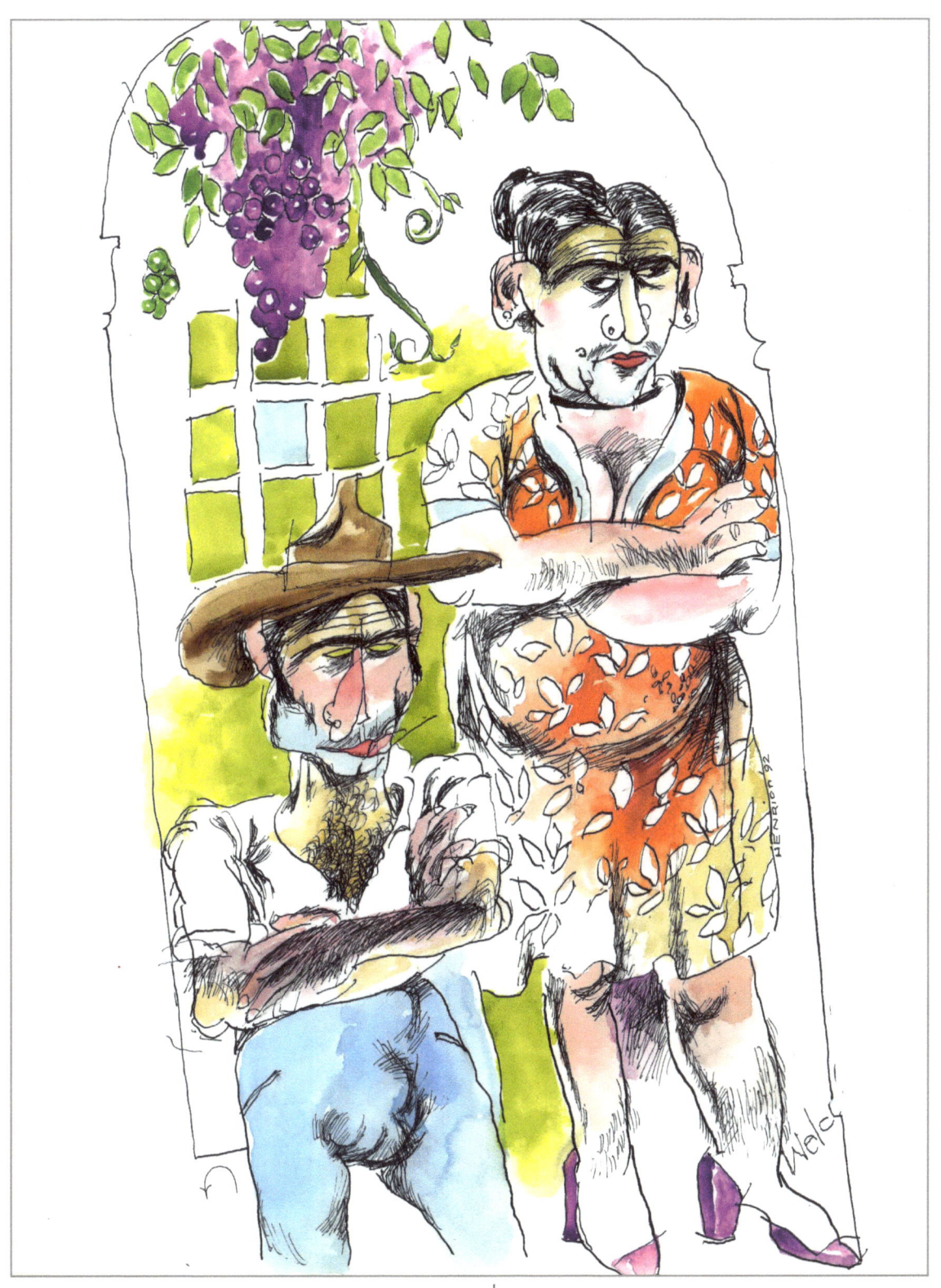

Couple

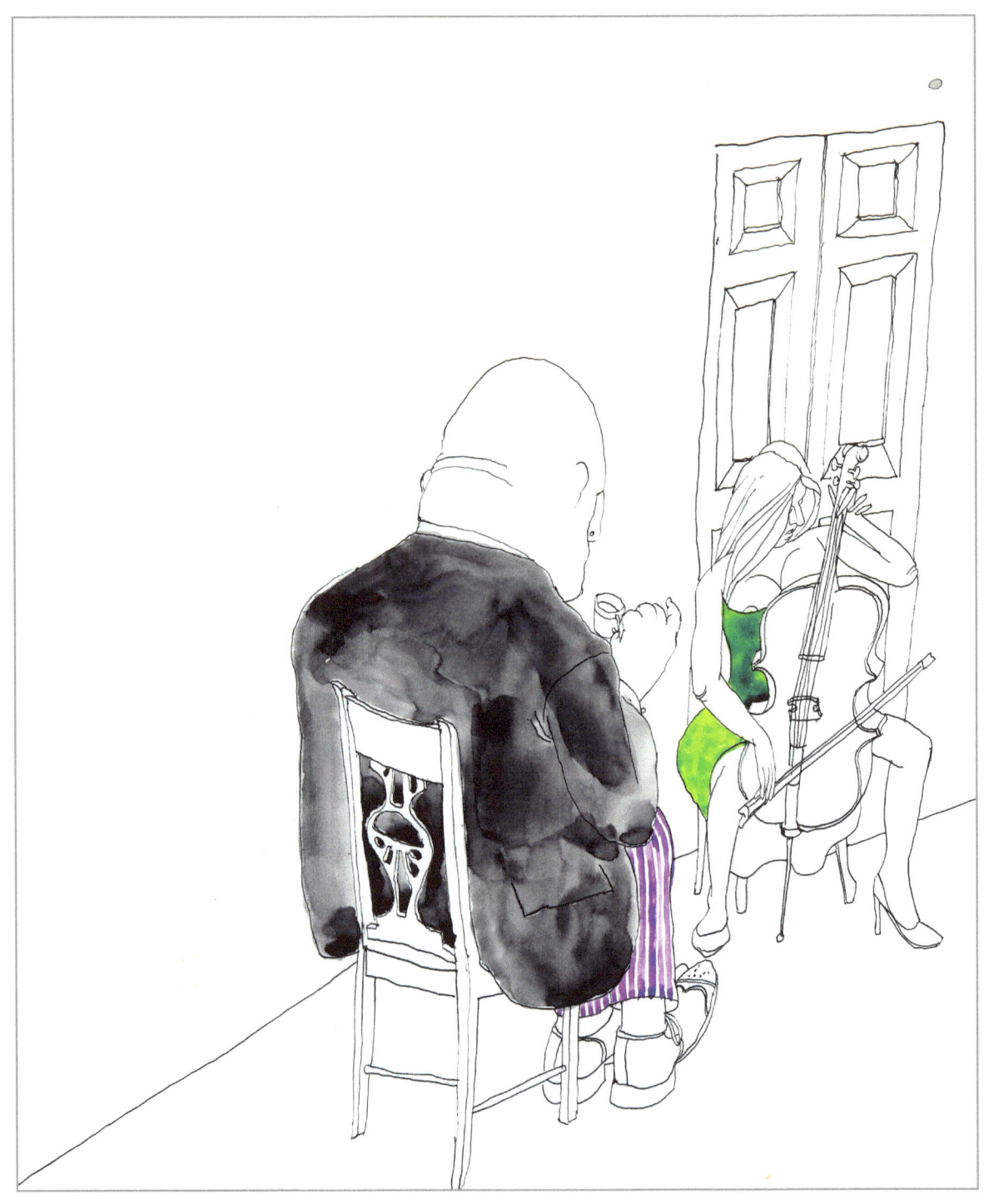

Music Lover 1

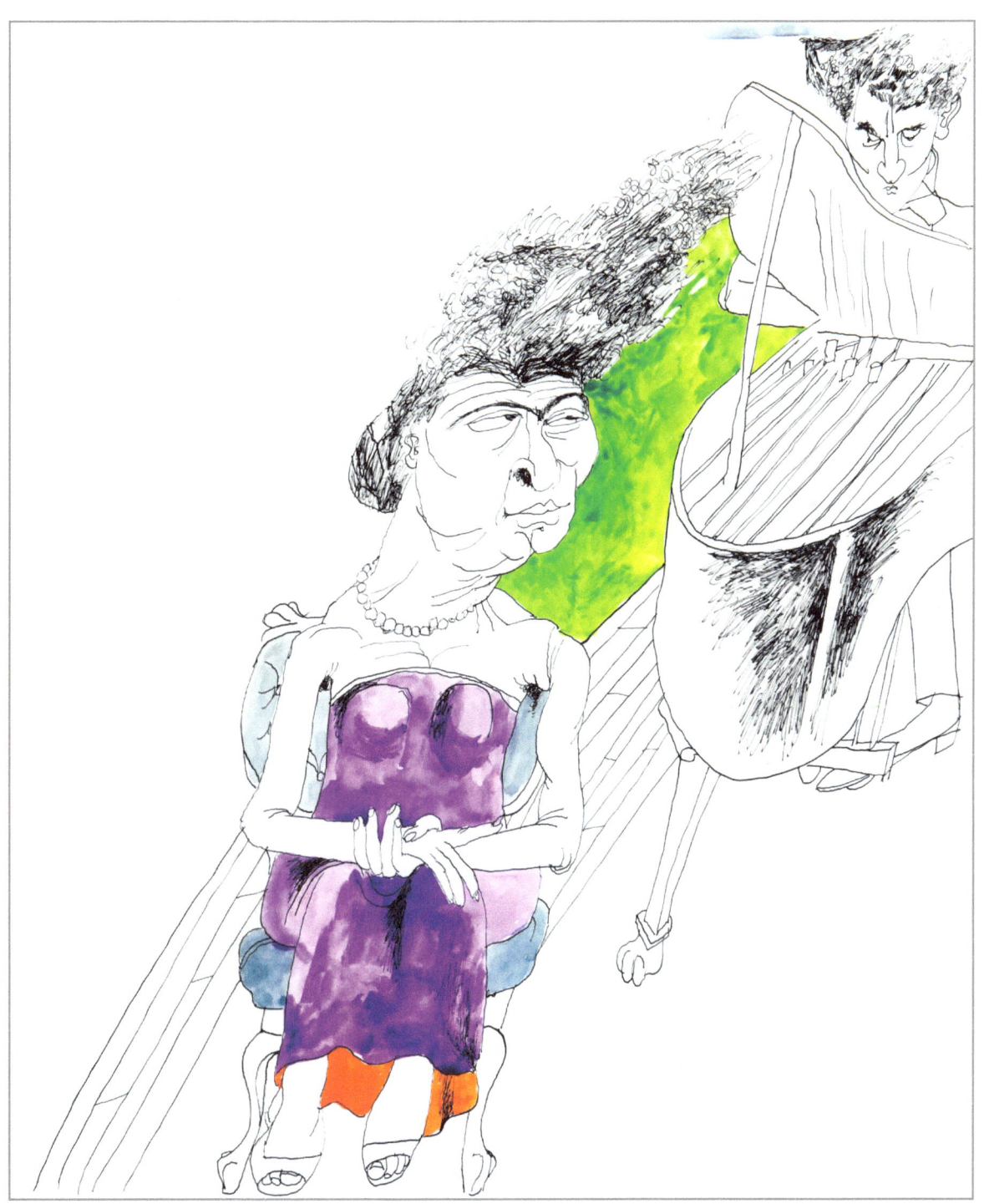

Music Lover 2

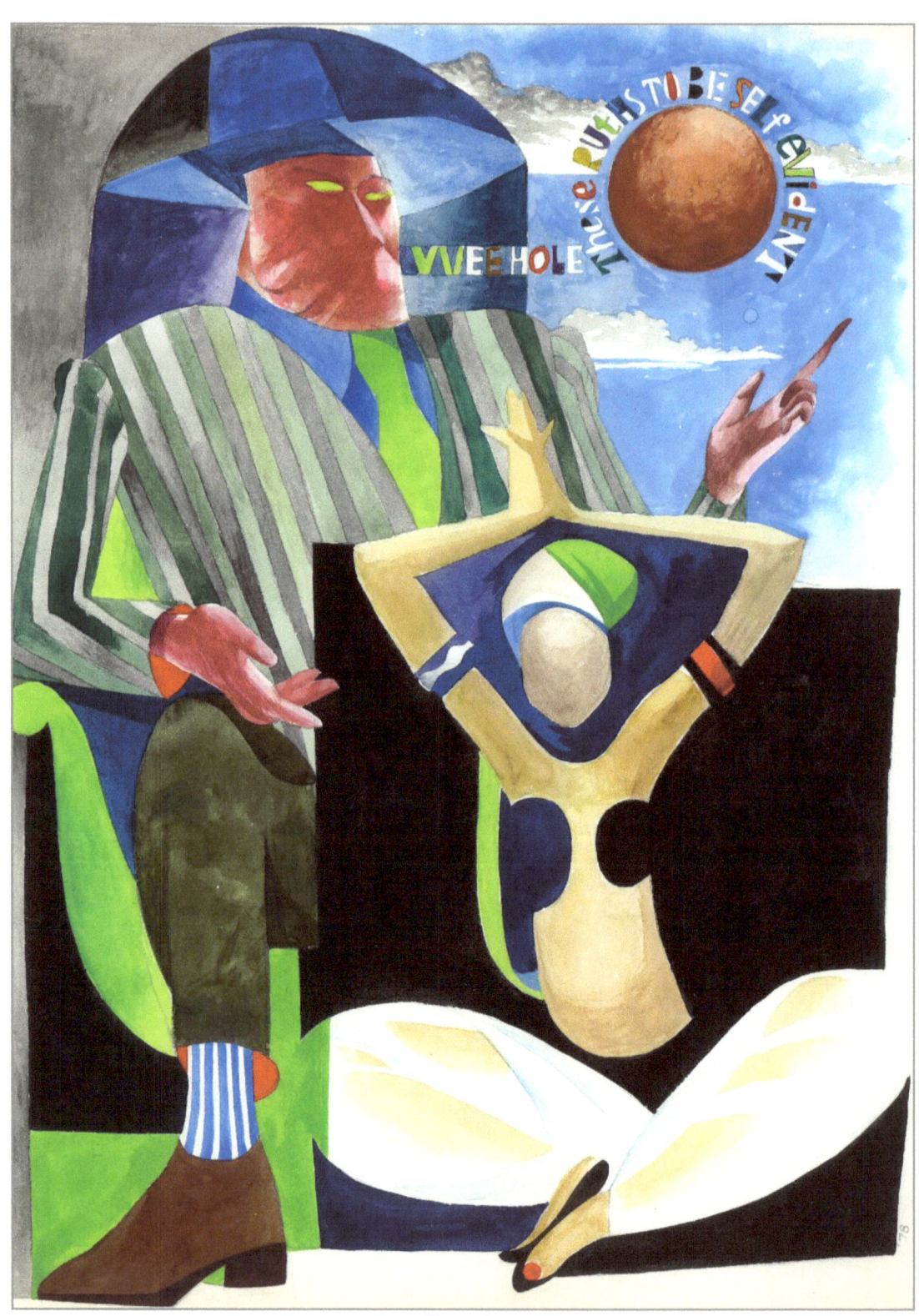

Self Evident

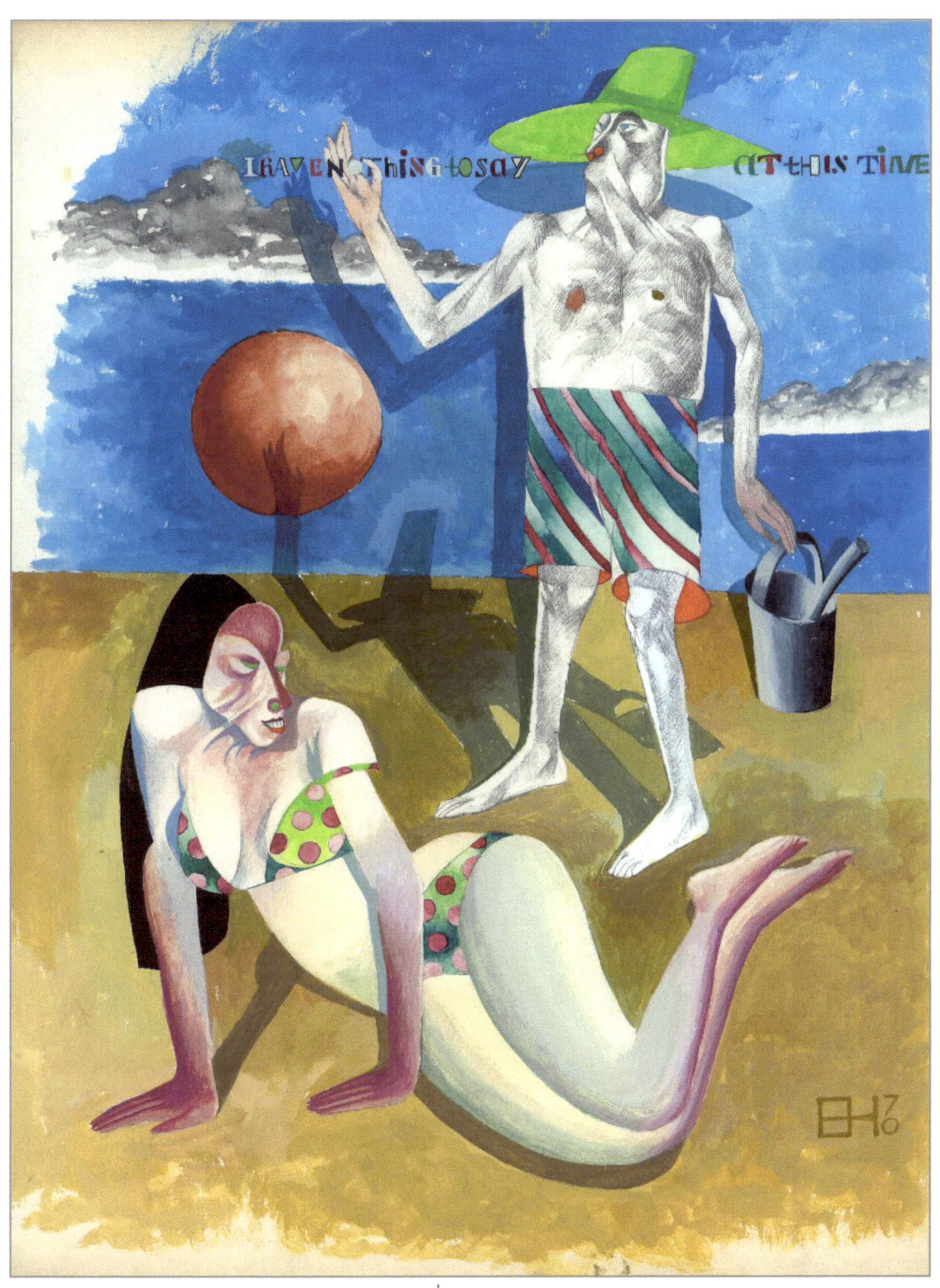

Nothing To Say

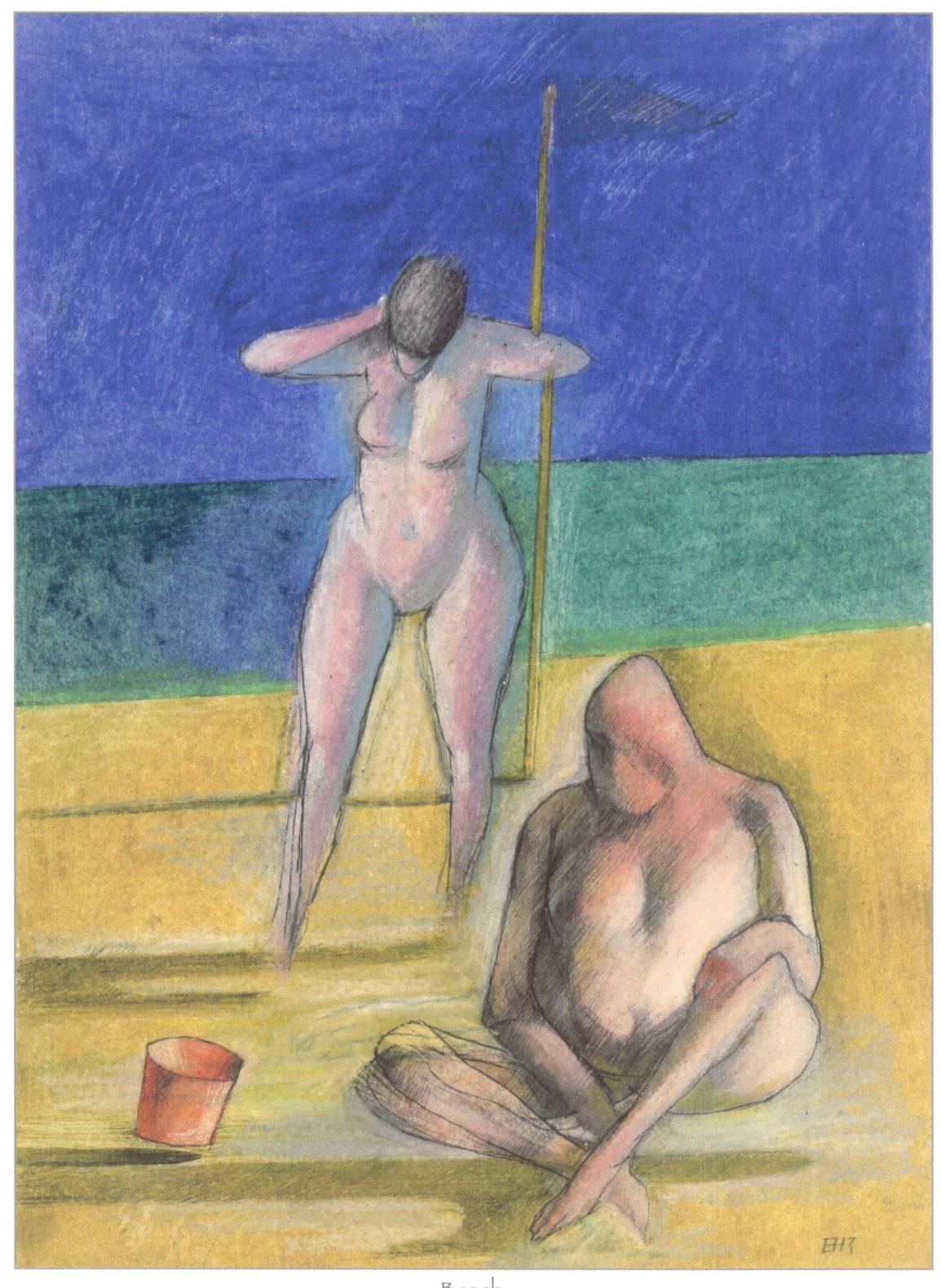

Beach

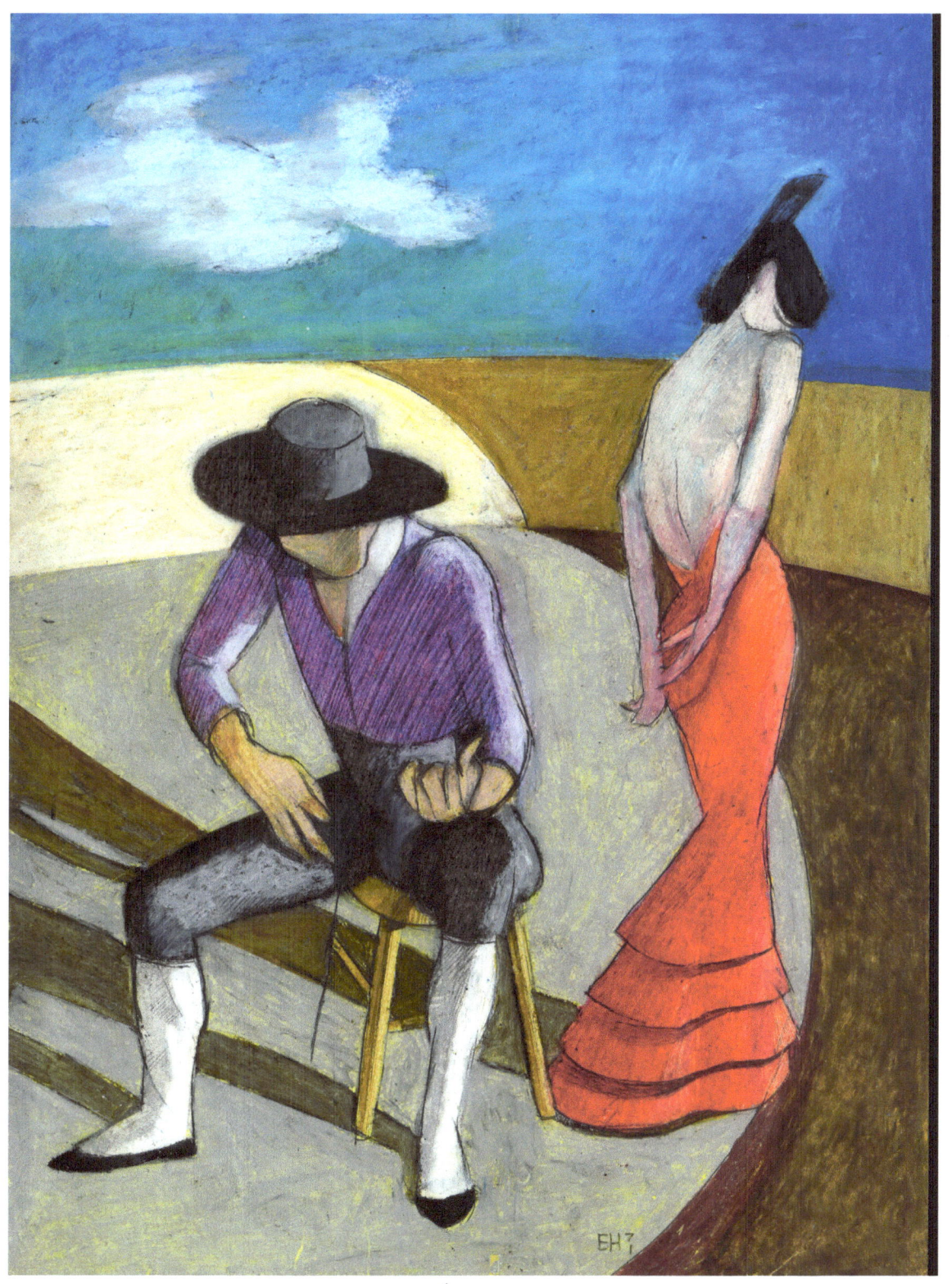

Flamenco

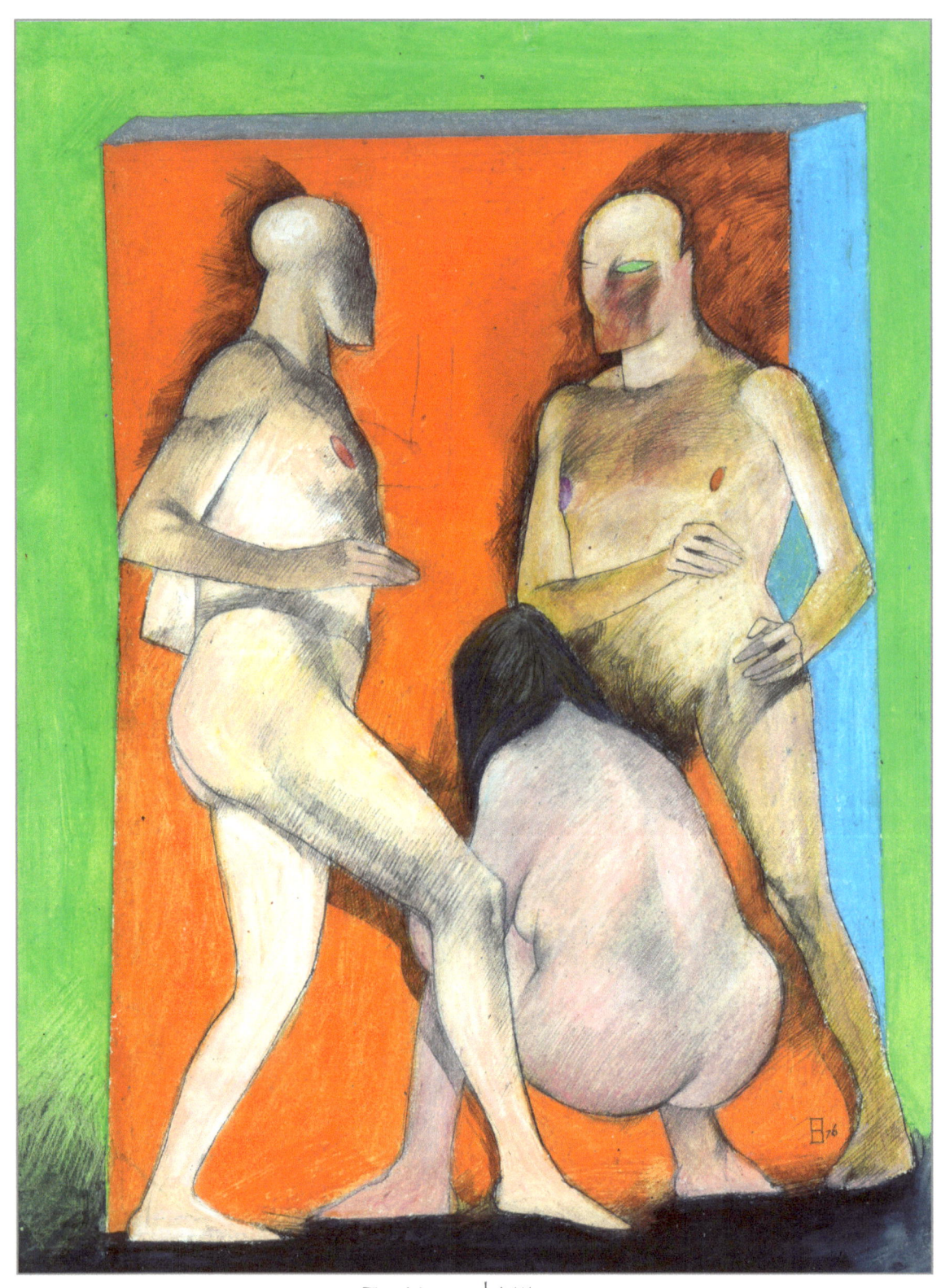

Two Men and A Woman

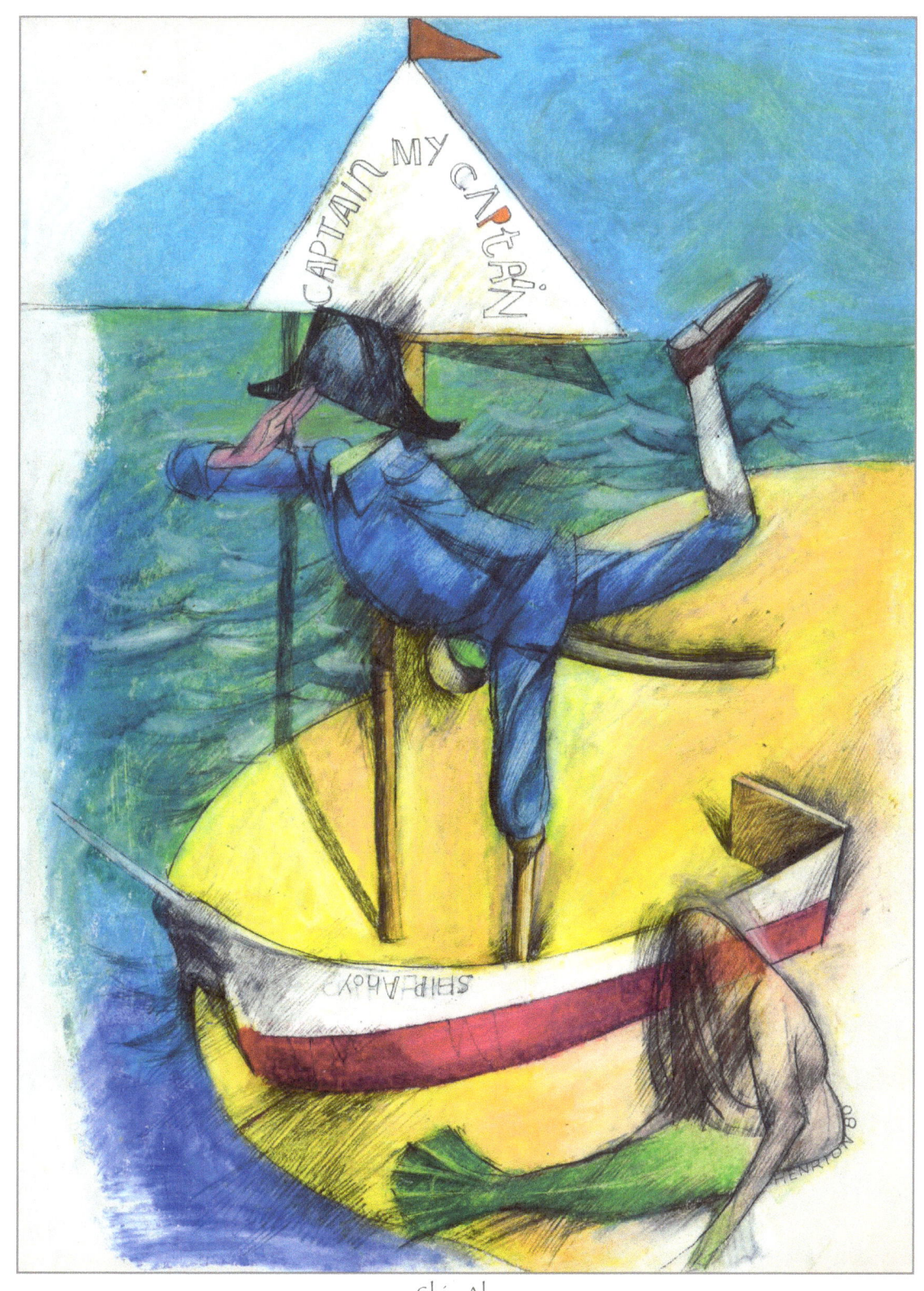

Ship Ahoy

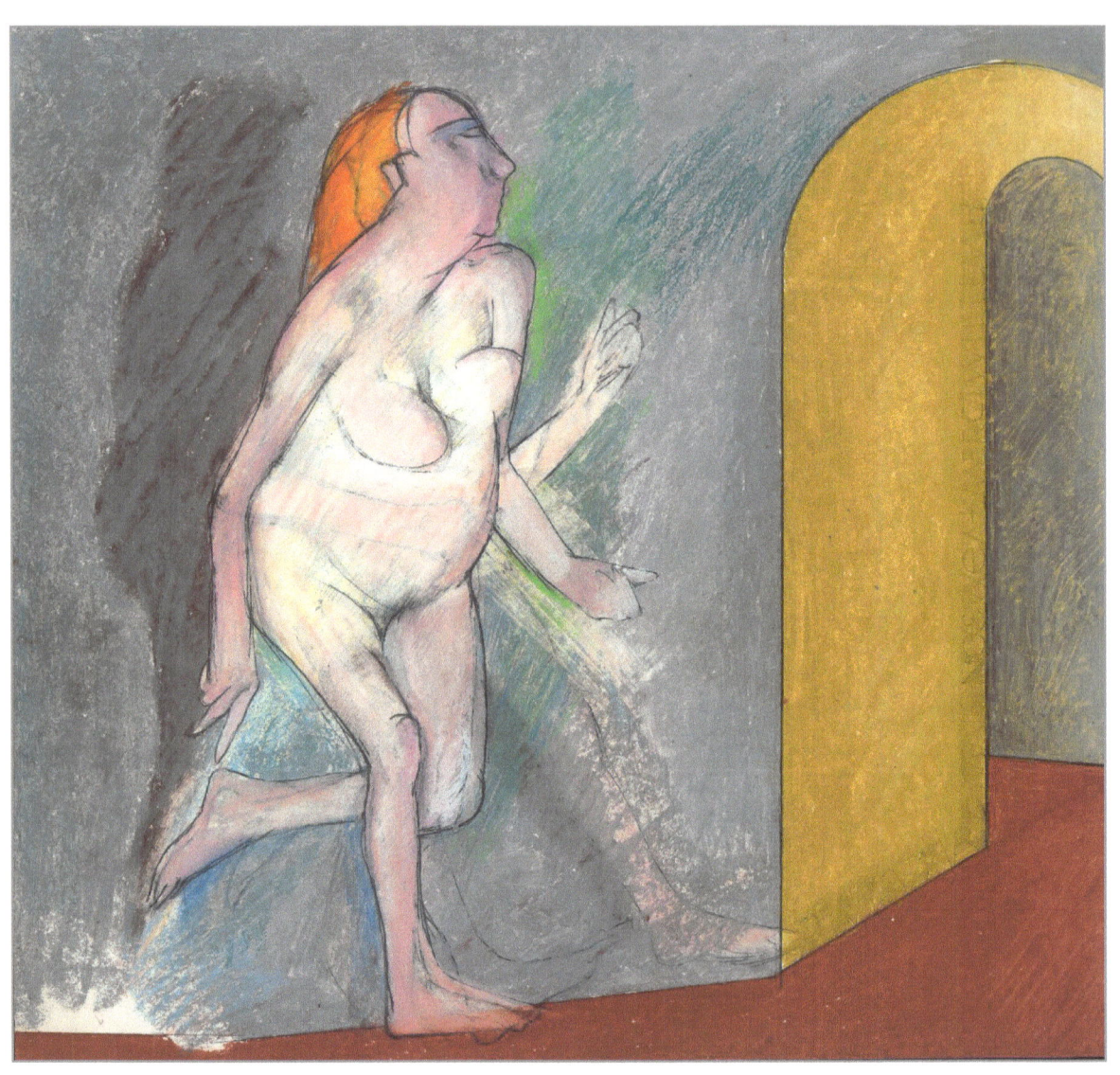

Running 1

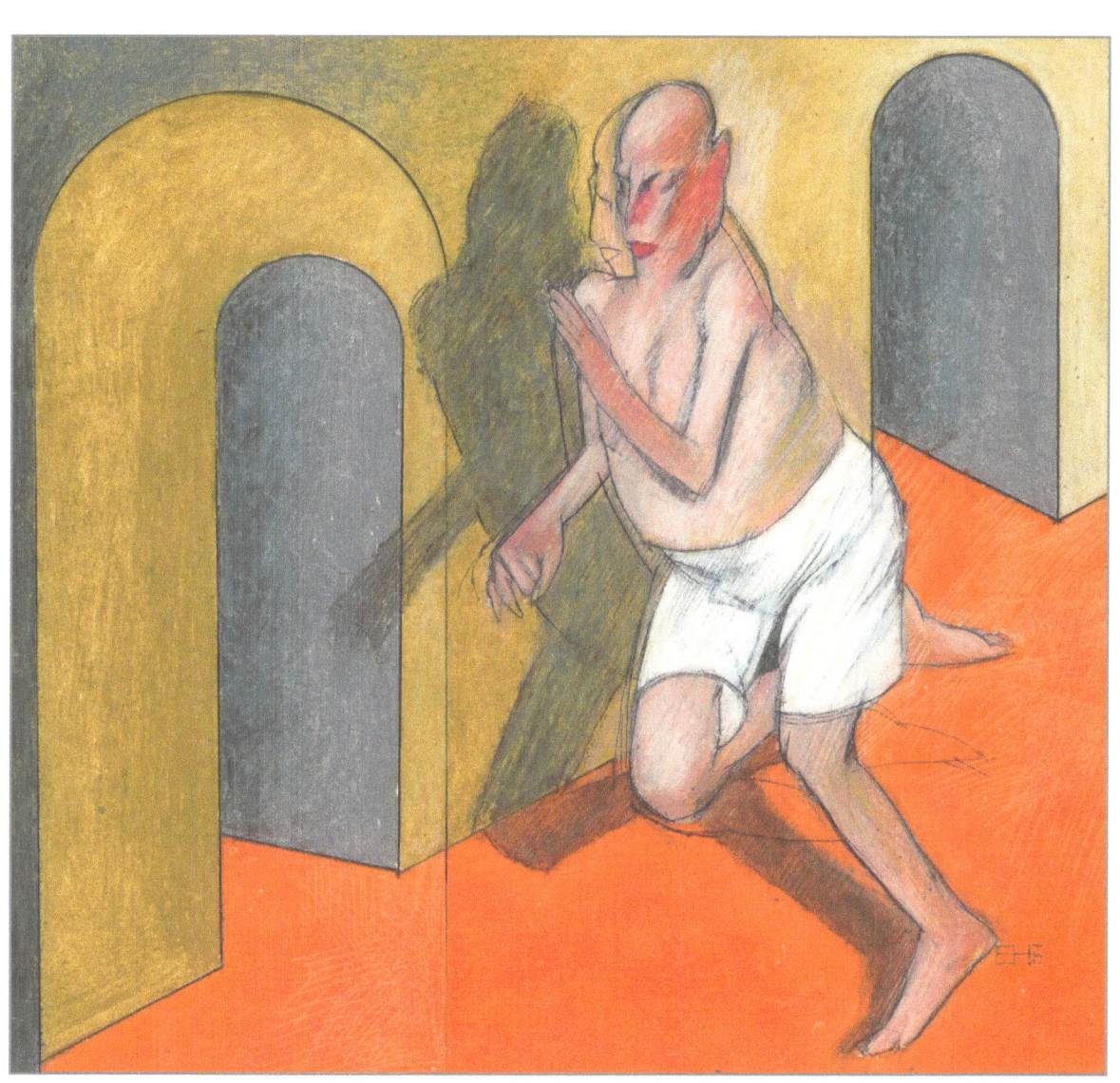

Running 2

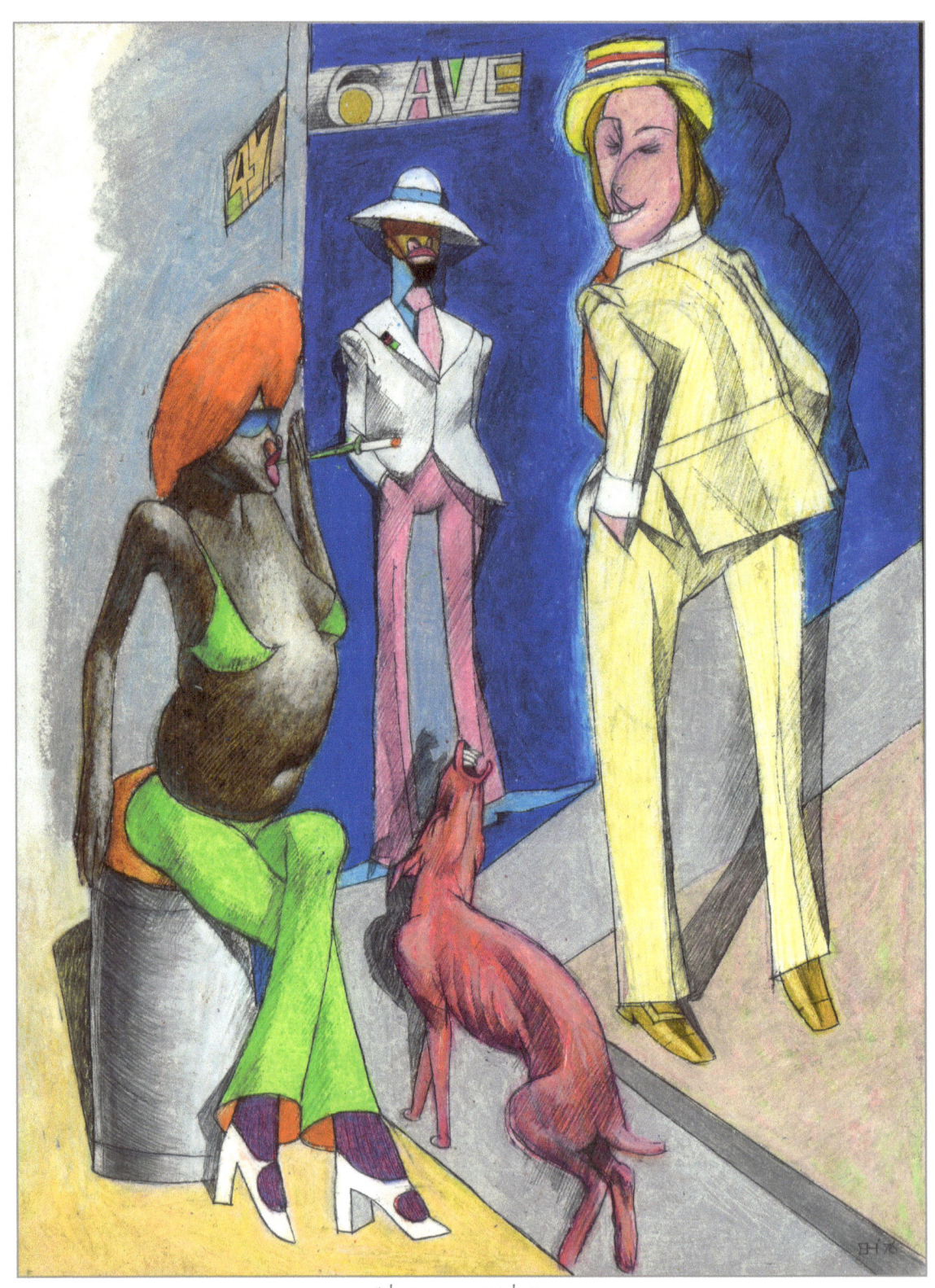

6th Avenue With Dog

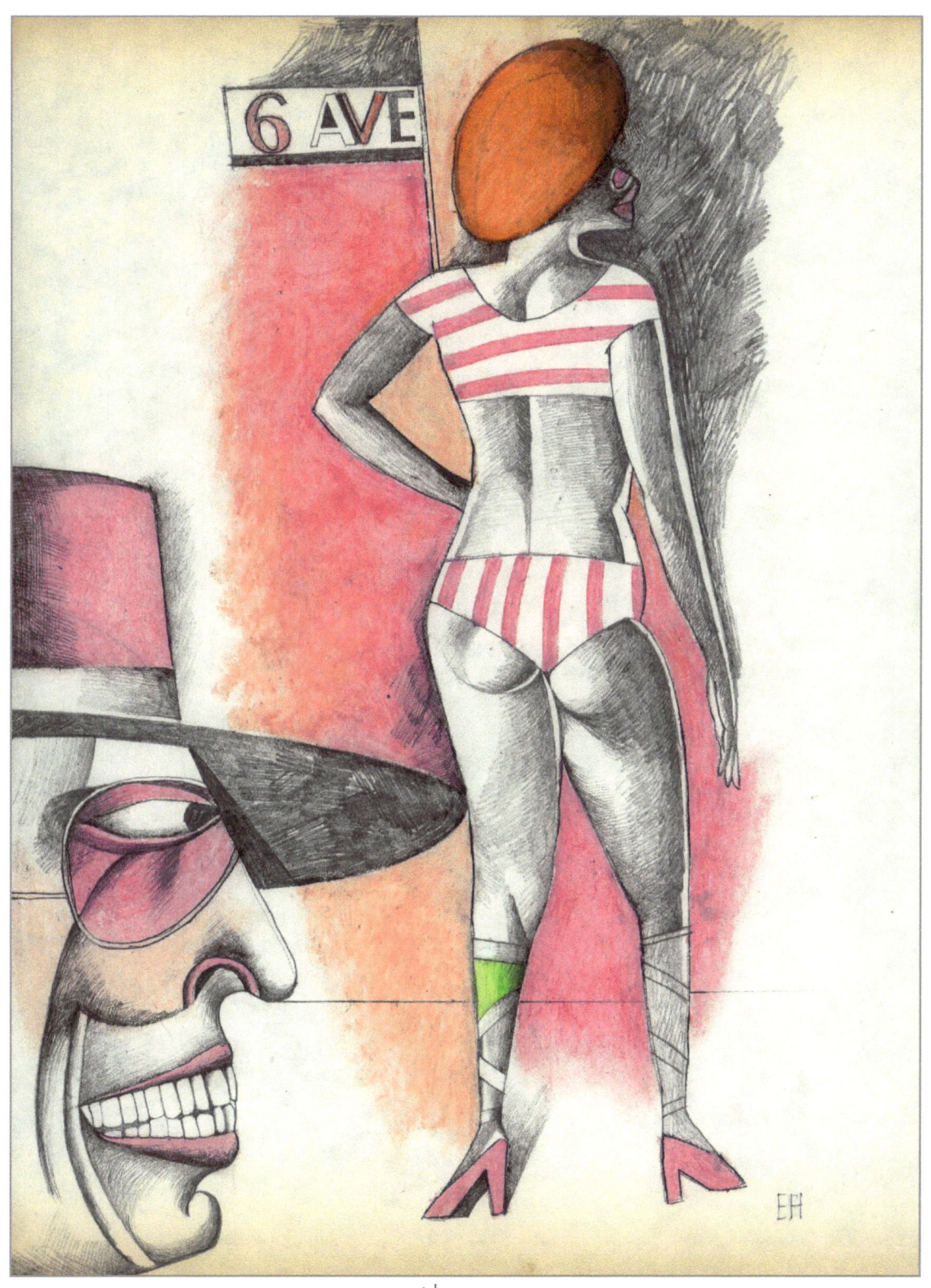

6th Avenue

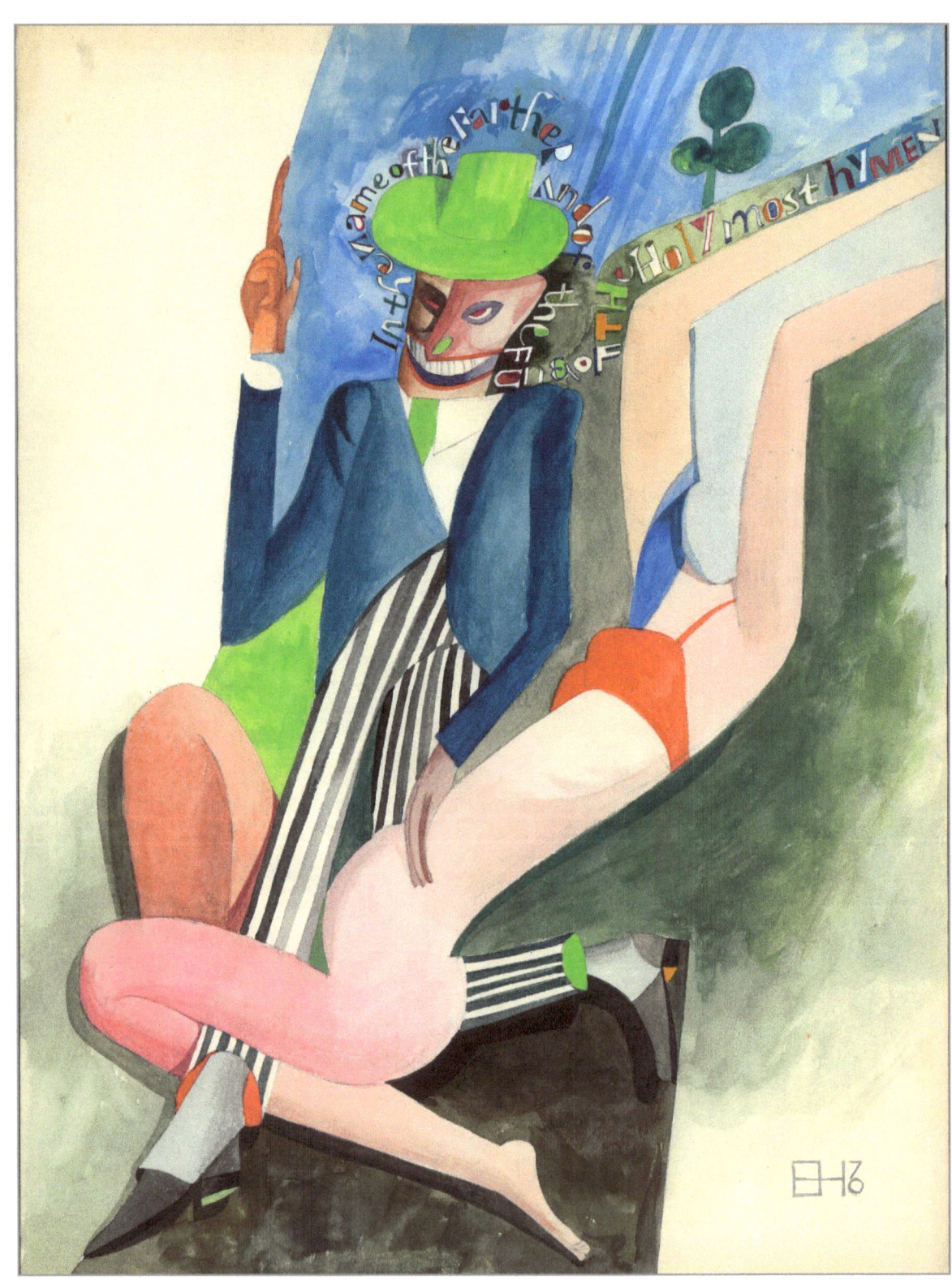

Baptism

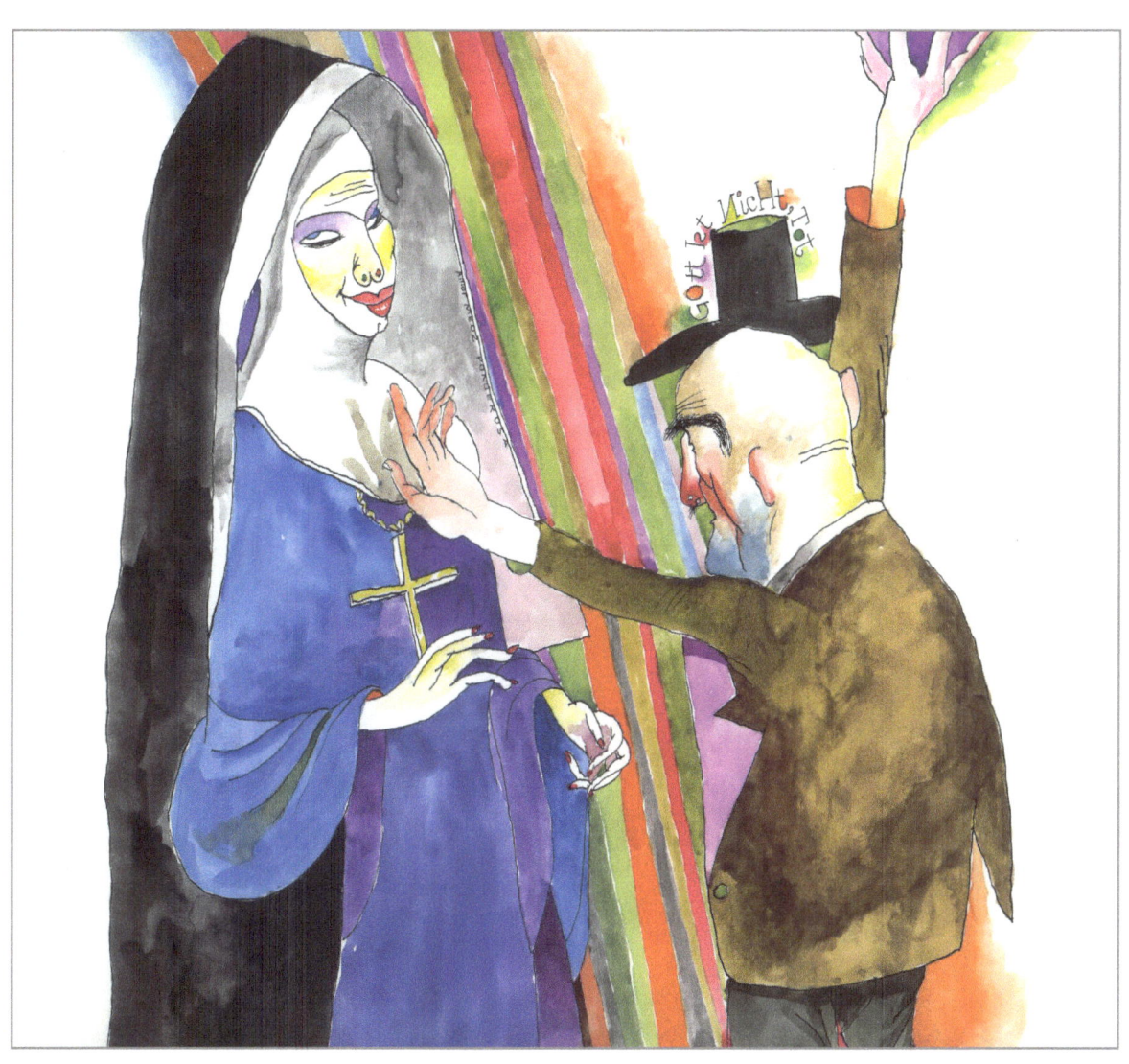

Heaven Sent

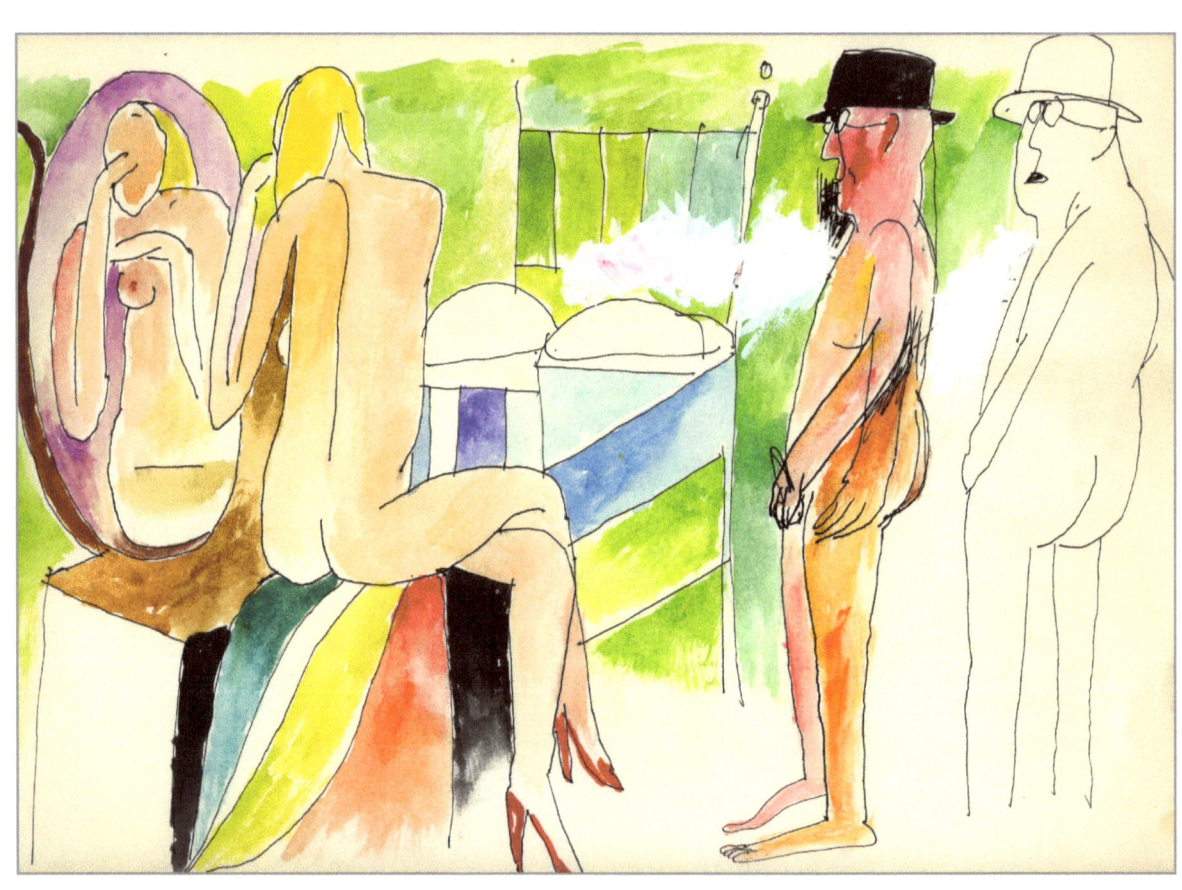

Haunting Me

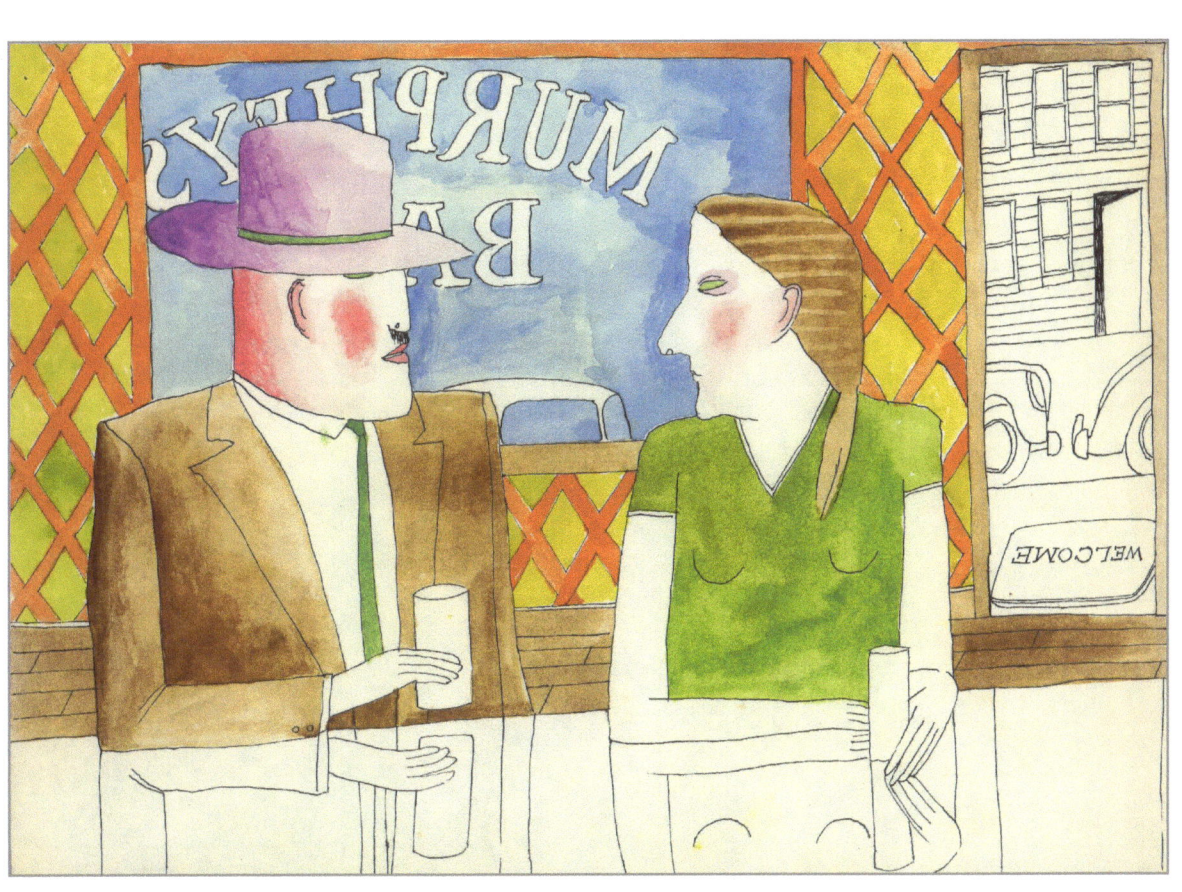

Murphy's Bar

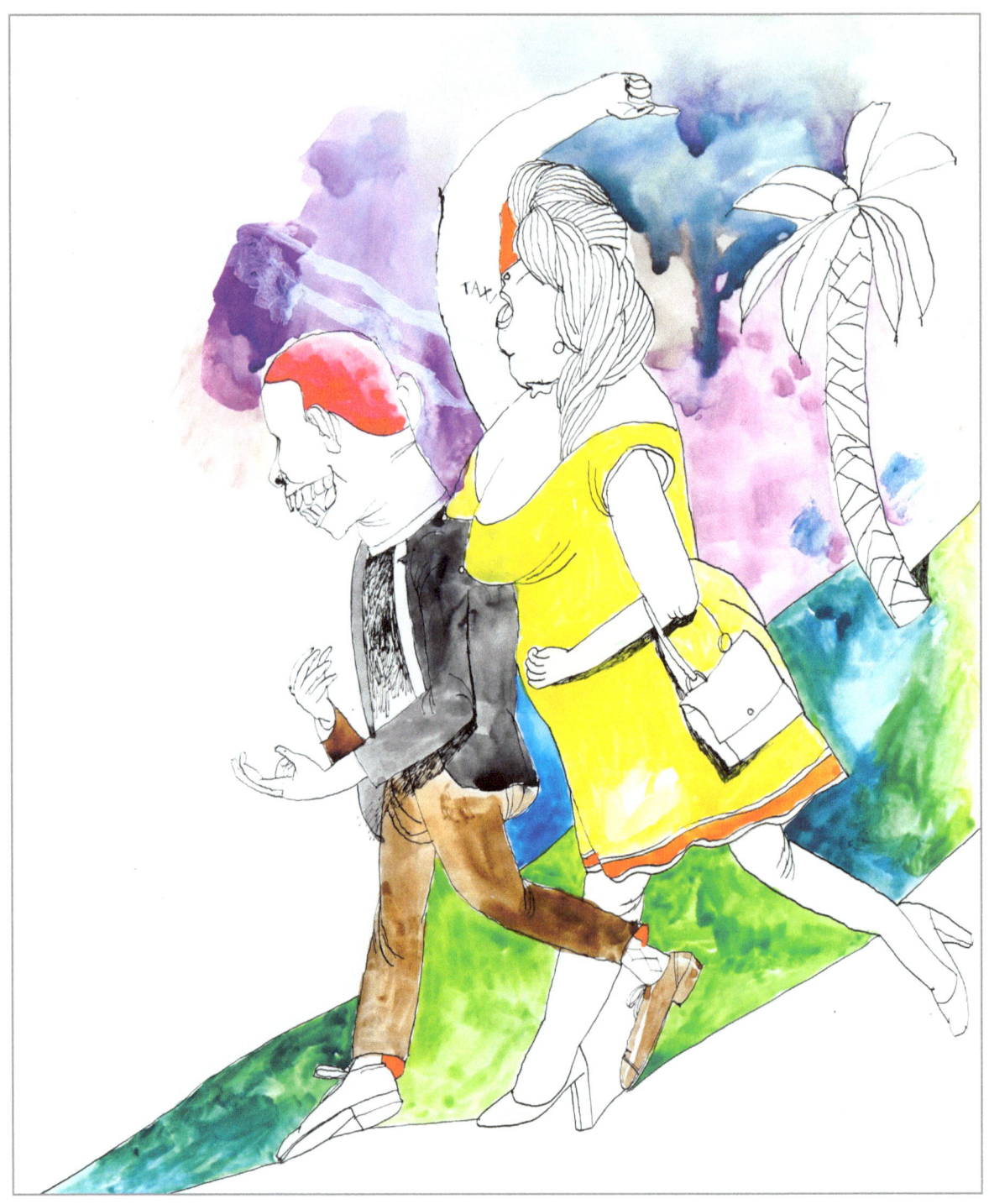

Taxi

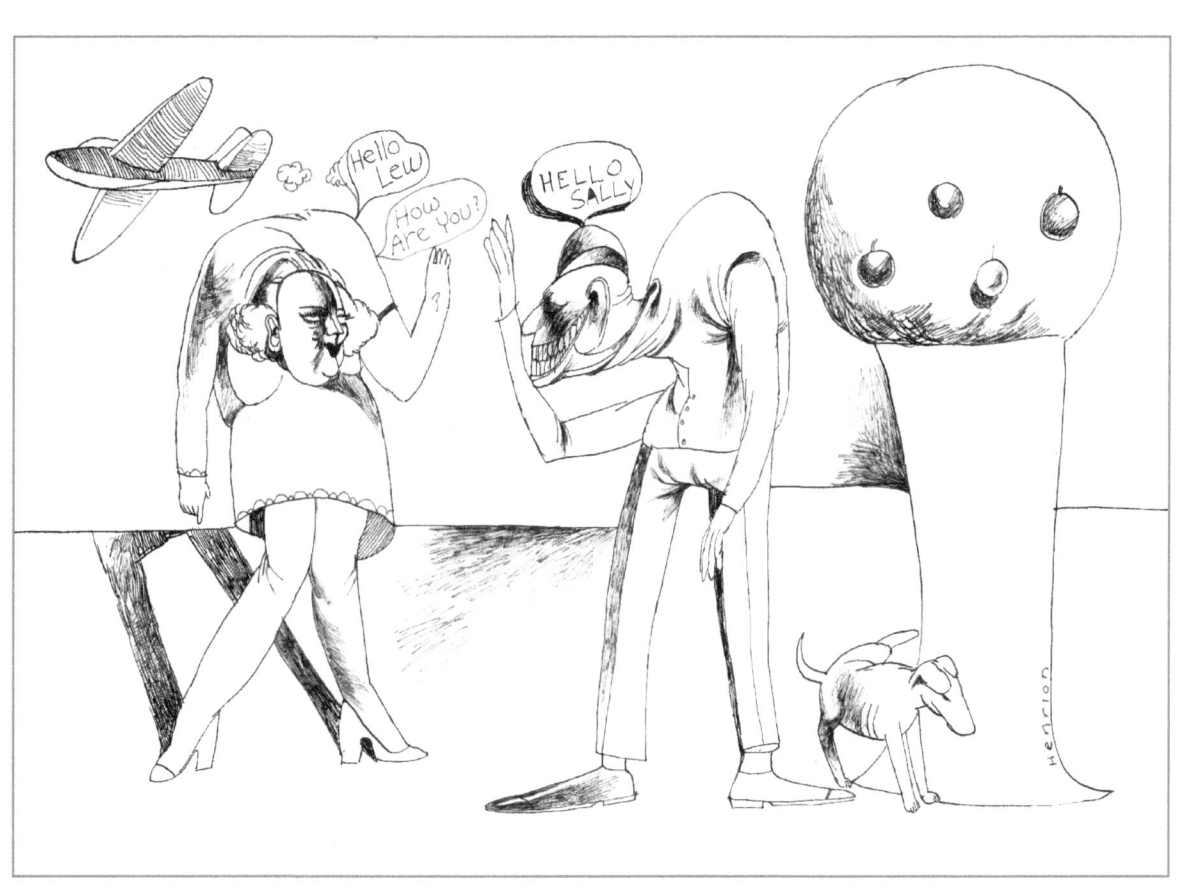

Hello

BIOGRAPHY

Ed Henrion grew up in Detroit Michigan. After studying painting with Alexander Zlatov-Mirsky in Chicago, he moved to New York in 1949 where he graduated from the Cooper Union College of Arts & Sciences in 1952. He has been living in Greenwich Village with his wife and fellow Cooper Union graduate, Marilyn Henrion, for over 60 years. Ed was a regular attendee at the 8th Street Artists' Club during the 1950's, along with the major abstract expressionist painters Motherwell, deKooning, Rothko, Barnett Newman, etc. During the 1960's and 70's the Henrions were immersed in the the art and literary scene of the time. Their social network included Joseph Cornell, Tom Wesselman, and Claes Oldenburg, in whose Happenings Marilyn performed. Salons held at their Greenwich Village apartment featured poetry readings by important poets of the day such as Howard Hart, Allen Ginsberg, Philip Lamantia, Bob Nichols, and Ray Bremser, as well as performances by avant garde composer, Jackson Maclow. Ed's satirical drawings constitute a no-holds-barred commentary on the New York scene as he lived it during a significant era. However, except for occasional freelance editorial illustrations for publications such as Human Events and Libertarian Review, he studiously avoided any involvement in the business of art. Instead, while continuing to create new drawings and paintings, Ed earned his living as an art teacher at Erasmus High School in Brooklyn, NY before retiring in 1987. Now an avid chess player and science enthusiast , he has finally relented in allowing his wife to introduce his extraordinary body of work to the public. These works have never before been exhibited or published.

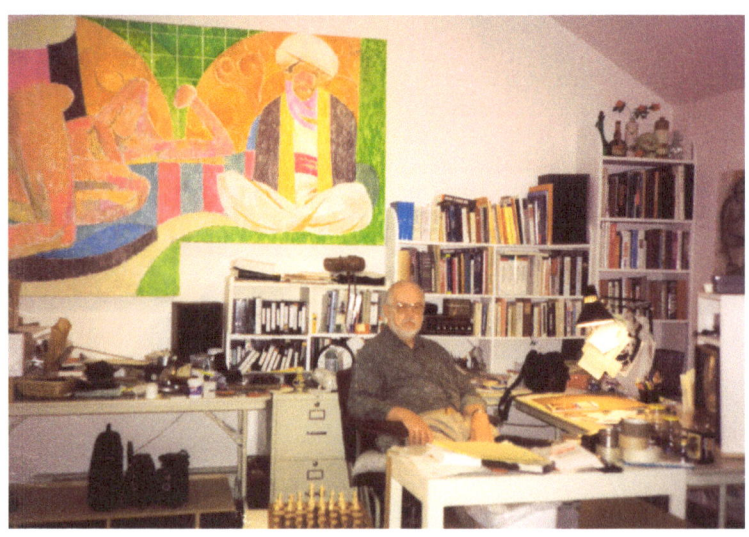

Book designed by Marilyn Henrion

www.ingramcontent.com/pod-product-compliance
Lightning Source LLC
Chambersburg PA
CBHW050824180526
45159CB00004B/1782